Be Gentle
Ten Ways to Bring Peace to Yourself and Others

by Donald Gallehr

DORRANCE
PUBLISHING CO
EST. 1920
PITTSBURGH, PENNSYLVANIA 15238

Dorrance Publishing Co
585 Alpha Drive
Pittsburgh, PA 15238
Visit our website at *www.dorrancebookstore.com*

ISBN: 978-1-6461-0791-9
eISBN: 978-1-6461-0692-9

Introduction

My two sons, ages eight and six, were walking across our front yard ahead of me when one punched the other in the shoulder. I had heard them talking. I had the sense that they were disagreeing about something, but I was too far behind them to know what they were saying. So, I called out to them, "Hey, hey—be gentle," and that was it. They proceeded to play together in the backyard for the rest of the afternoon, swinging on the swing and sloshing down the slide. No punching, no arguing, no fighting.

When I look back on this event, I am well aware that my few words to them were in a much larger context. I was not the kind of parent who spanked them or yelled at them. Instead, I held them in my arms and placed them on the floor when they asked to get down. I played with them and each night I picked up their toys and placed them back on the shelves in the den. I listened to them and held real conversations with them. Because I was a young teacher at the time, our family of three children and two adults had very little money. In fact, I was surprised one day to see my late wife giving the kids bread and butter sandwiches for lunch. We didn't have enough money for peanut butter, bologna, or cheese. But we loved our children and showed it in countless ways.

Without bragging, I can say I worked very hard to be at a point where I could say, "Be gentle," and have it make an impact on my children. First of all, I had to be gentle with myself. If I had been harsh or cruel with myself, my simple admonition would not have worked with my children. If I had not done countless things each day to bring myself to a state of gentleness, love, and compassion, I could not have treated them in a manner that enabled them to treat themselves, each other, and those they came into contact with in the same way.

The "countless things" I did each day, plus several that I learned in the years after my daughter and two sons left the nest, I have consolidated into ten ideas that form the ten chapters of this book. Even though this book is also a self-help memoir, I hope it will inspire you, my reader, to be just as gentle with yourself and others as I was that day with my two sons.

Before going any further, there is something I need to tell you about myself. I am, by nature, a person who understates. Being gentle sounds easy, but getting to that stage is hard as hell. When I say it requires countless acts throughout the day, I mean it.

Another thing you need to know is that all ten steps are interrelated. I can't gain the benefits of letting go of the garbage in my head if I don't actually do it and to get the time in a busy day to focus and let go, I have to give up something else. I've tried "Oh, I'll do it tomorrow," but it doesn't work. "Oh, this works just as well," doesn't cut it either. I can't be gentle to someone if, on the inside for totally unrelated reasons, I feel like pushing him off a cliff. I have to take care of myself first, and then I can take care of others.

I recommend that you read this book one section at a time and if you're interested, try out each step. You may also find it helpful to keep track of your thoughts and actions in a journal or private notebook where you can be honest with yourself about how you're treating yourself, your loved ones, and those you come into contact with throughout your day. In addition, I also recommend that you get someone to take this journey with you—a "Be Gentle" buddy. Make sure it is someone who has your best interests at heart, someone who will help you out when that's what you need, as well as someone who will let you fall on your face if that's the best way for you to learn.

You will notice that some of these steps are pretty common and have been around for a long time. In the information age, there is no lack of advice on how to live a wonderful life. The challenge is applying this knowledge to ourselves so that we make our lives the very best they can be. There is plenty of brain research, philosophy, and psychology to back up these ten steps and I encourage you to cross traditional boundaries every chance you get in order to add depth to your understanding and breadth to your practice. I've placed an appendix at the end of the book to list, by chapter, the articles, books, and research that I refer to throughout this book. These will give you greater depth of understanding of these ten steps that I think you will find helpful.

Finally, feel free to add some steps of your own. Just jot them down when you get a chance and add them to your practice.

Be assured that in spirit I am with you every step of the way. I, too, am your "Be Gentle" buddy.

Chapter 1

LET GO OF I CAN'T, I SHOULD, I WANT, I NEED

In 1989, my three children had left the nest, each one going off to college to build lives of their own. Like many parents, I missed them terribly and because they had become the center of my life for the previous twenty-three years, I was looking at the future as if it had nothing in it for me. Yes, it was the Empty Nest Syndrome, a Mid-Life Crisis, and no doubt a host of other things. One day I looked in the mirror and said, "He's one lost puppy!"

So, I spent a year doing a lot of meditating because for me meditation was a way to regain the peace and love I had become accustomed to when my children were at home. I kept my teaching job and most of the people around me had no idea I was going through a tough time. Then, one evening, I went to bed feeling completely lost—only to wake up in the middle of the night with three directives in my head:

> Let go of "I can't," "I should," "I want," "I need".
> See things as they are, not as I would have them.
> Help things become what they were meant to be.

I had no idea where these three directives came from or what I was to do with them, but I wrote them down so I wouldn't forget them.

In the years that followed, I worked on letting go of "I can't," "I should," "I want," and "I need" and in this chapter I'll show you what I did, and still do, and hopefully it will help you when you confront these four dictates. I'll be referring to my practice of meditation throughout this whole book and I'll focus on it specifically in chapter four. But for now, let me say that when I meditate at least once a day, I find it much easier to let go of these four things. When I skip a day or more of meditation, they come back to rule the roost. As you will see as you move through all ten chapters, the practice of doing something I recommend in one chapter also supports the practice of doing things I talk about in the other chapters.

Letting Go of "I Can't"

Actually, the process of letting go of these four dictates is identical to the first part of just about any meditation practice. For instance, when I have an "I can't" thought, I label it— "This is one of those 'I can't' thoughts," hold it for several moments, and then let it go. I find the act of labeling to be an important step after recognizing that a thought is taking hold of my mind and by now labeling is relatively simple for me. There are, after all, a zillion thoughts in my head, but most of them fit under a limited number of categories. Of course, when I let go of one of these thoughts, another one arrives. But I have an easier time letting go of the second one and an even easier time letting go of the third one because I have let go of the first two. Yes, some days, especially when I am doing yard work or painting the house, I am surprised by the repetition of thoughts and I'll say to myself, "I thought I had released you months ago," or "I just let go of you ten minutes

2

ago. What the hell are you doing here? Go away!" It's true for all of us that recognizing a thought, labeling it, and letting it go is essential if we're to create a calm and clear mind.

By the way, one of my friends who knew I was writing a book called *Be Gentle* asked me why I thought it was at all important to be gentle.

I told her, "It's about achieving inner peace. On an individual level, it is what humans are meant to be, just as we're meant to be healthy and happy."

She then asked, "Why is that important?"

I replied, "For me it's very important—not just on an individual level, but on a world-wide level as well. People who are at peace with themselves bring peace to others and in the long term we're talking about bringing peace to the world."

Her question made me realize that not all people care about peace, yet at the same time it reminded me of people I've met who are at peace with themselves and they do bring peace to others.

Let me to go into a little more detail about the act of letting go. First of all, I don't know if all children grow up with "I can't" and "I should" rattling in their heads, but I did. For me, they were constant companions. They came from my parents, my teachers, and other authority figures. As we all know, there are times when telling a youngster "No, you can't play with matches in the house," is just plain smart. Yes, we want people to learn from experience, but we don't want them to burn down the house in the process.

Another example of "I can't" is changing the oil in my car. I used to change it all by myself and if I really had to I could do it again I could. But at this stage in my life, it makes much more sense for me to take my car in and have the oil changed by someone who can also tell at a glance that I need new brake pads on my front wheels.

And finally, an example of an "I can't" that I still struggle with is, "I can't be the last one out of the house." Where does this come from for me? Probably from my older brother and sister going off to college and leaving me behind. I still don't like being left behind, but I just have to learn to be comfortable being myself wherever I am.

Before moving on, I want to give you one example of how I recently let go of an "I can't" thought. On one morning, my cat woke me by scratching the bed only inches from my hand. He does this every day and it is his way of asking me to let him out. I glanced at the clock on the bedside table to make sure it was close to 7:00 AM and then glanced out the window to see if there was enough light to let him out. There was. So now the only question was the temperature. I slid out of bed, followed him down the stairs, and walked into the kitchen to read the thermometer hanging outside the window. It read 38 degrees. I took one more look outside and then turned to my cat who turned his head to look me straight in the eye and I knew exactly what he was thinking: "Please, please. Can I go out now?"

"No, not yet," I said. "It's still too cold and it's not quite bright enough yet. Let's wait till it gets a little brighter and a little warmer." I leaned down and petted him on the head.

He gave me a look of mild disappointment and walked over to his cat food.

I looked up at the kitchen clock. It was 6:52 AM. I was much too awake to go back to bed because I had already had almost eight hours of sleep. I then recalled that it was Sunday and I found myself thinking, *It's too early to work—especially on a Sunday.* I thought of several alternatives—checking the latest news on the internet, emptying the dishwasher, meditating for twenty minutes, getting the newspaper off the front lawn, working out… Then, all of a sudden, it hit me. Even though I had not phrased it as such, this was an "I can't" thought. Instead of acting on it, I stared right at it and it began to break apart.

Yes, 6:52 AM is early.

"You need to let go of this 'I can't' thought," I said to myself. "Yes, it's Sunday and yes, for many people it is a day of rest." Surprisingly, that was it. What followed was a moment of profound peace and after that I worked for three hours without any problem.

Before moving on, please take a minute to jot down a few of the "I can't" thoughts that come into your life. If you like, also take a minute to select one and just look at it to see what happens.

Letting Go of "I Should"

We all have "I should" thoughts and we need to label them as such, look at them, then let them go so that we have more options and can see things in a larger context.

One of the "I should" thoughts I still at times struggle with is being on time. If my wife and I say we're leaving the house at 6:15, I create an "I should" thought. Of course, it doesn't always make sense to do this. Sometimes it's better for me to give my wife enough time to take a shower and dress so that she looks beautiful than it is for me to rush her. When I let go of my "I should" thought, I easily find important things that I can do to fill the time and my wife is happy with me too.

One of the "should" thoughts that were part of my generation in the 1950s was, "children should be seen, not heard." As a result, I and many of my peers had very few real conversations with our parents, teachers, or adults. This dictate, of course, changed when I was raising my children and most parents in the 1960s and later had countless meaningful conversations with their children.

Of course, there are many "should" thoughts that make sense, including "you shouldn't drink and drive." Rarely does a day go by when we don't hear of an accident being caused by drunk driving. "I should be sober if I'm going to drive" should be a thought in everyone's mind, and one that we all follow. When we label this thought and let it go, we see the larger picture—our loved ones and those around us who will be impacted if we have an accident. We have a moral obligation to ourselves and to others to drive safely. Refusing to drink and drive gives us the opportunity to influence the behavior of others in a very positive way.

The next time an "I should" or "I shouldn't" thought comes to you, label it, let it go, and open your eyes to the larger picture. I think you'll really like what you see.

Letting Go of "I Want" and "I Need"

I wrote the earliest version of this book sitting in Borders—yes, before they closed. Some may think this strange because I have an office at work and an office at home, but what this bookstore had that my offices did not is people. For me, people are part of both my "I want" list and my "I need" list.

How do I know this? If I go for several days without seeing people, I lose energy and become despondent, moping around the house. When I teach class, attend meetings, have friends over, share my day with my wife, Ceres, run into neighbors on the street or fellow handymen in the hardware store—I meet my basic desire to be around people. In fact, when I teach, I am so happy and even the time I spend preparing for class is fulfilling because I am thinking about my students. Can I survive without people? Yes, but it will feel like solitary confinement and that's why I placed it number five on my wants and needs list.

To a degree, all humans share basic wants and needs and here I am going to use Abraham Maslow's 1943 "A Theory of Human Motivation" as a point of reference. Maslow spoke of five levels of needs in his hierarchy, with the most basic level being our physiological need for water, air, food, and sleep. It's hard to argue about these four. In fact, removing them from our lives is the same as ending our lives.

The first part that I want to focus on is what happens when we don't get one of these four. Let's talk about food—perhaps the most problematic of the four in recent times. There have been countless books dealing with poverty and starvation, as well as countless books dealing with overeating and obesity. When it comes to dieting, many of the books deal with reducing calories. As you may already know, for many overeaters the crucial point is listening to the body we are feeding. When we are hungry, the body is telling us—"Feed me, please, because I'm hungry." Of course we have to make sure we listen to our bodies and when we have not eaten for a long period of time, the body is right to speak up.

For our part, we need to respond not only by eating something— hopefully something that is nutritious and good for us—but also immediately after eating we need to listen to what our bodies are saying. Our bodies are quick responders to taste telling us such things as, "Oh, that's delicious," or "Yuck," but they are slow when it comes to telling us "That's enough." In fact, our bodies usually take about twenty minutes to get back to us with, "Oh, thank you so much. That's all I need." When we eat more than our bodies need, we're responding to our desires and at times that's not healthy. It's better for us to stop when our needs are satisfied.

Maslow goes on to talk about other needs such as security needs (having a job and living in a safe environment) and social needs (love and healthy relationships—even companionship or people as I mentioned above). He also refers to esteem needs that include self-esteem and social recognition and finally self-actualizing needs that include personal growth. In addition, people other than Maslow have listed clothing, sunlight, love, shelter, and sex as other human needs.

So, our first step is to honestly identify our wants and needs. The word "honestly" here is important. Yes, we'll all list water, air, food, and sleep, but from there on our lists will differ—and that's good. We are individuals and despite genes and the influence of others, we're all unique. In our being honest with ourselves, it's important that we draw a line between our wants and our needs and yes, these lines will be different for each of us. I have friends who don't want or need people. In fact, some of them are happier when they go for days without seeing people. As I mentioned, I'm just the opposite.

To help you, think of wants and needs you may have. Here are a few that I've seen in people: money/overall wealth, leading movements, friends/clubs, children/family, work/career, marriage/close relationships, travel/exploring new territories, and creating new things.

Please take a minute to make a list starting with your needs. Then go on to items that are both needs and wants and end with ones that are just desires.

You're back. Just so that you know that I do the things I ask of you, here is my most current list which starts with my needs and then gradually goes on to my desires. As I said earlier, people for me are both needs and desires:

- Water
- Air
- Food
- Sleep
- People
- Love
- Personal Growth
- Helping Others
- Teaching
- Sex
- Intelligence

If you are doing this with a friend or a group, please take a minute to share your list with them and listen as they share their lists with you.

Now we can talk about listening to some of these needs. We all need air, but how often do we actually pay attention to our breathing? In fact, if someone came up to us and asked, "What are you doing?" and we said, "Breathing," that person would probably think us weird. But try it. Just breathe in and breath out—feel the air come into your nose and down into your lungs and then feel the air leave your nose. It may not be the greatest sensation you've ever experienced, but I'm guessing that it's at least satisfying. Why am I asking you to do this? So that we can take the next step and let go of our needs, something at this point that you may think is really crazy.

We can't be free, nor can we be happy, if we're constantly living in the future trying to meet our needs or living in the past wishing we had. Once we are present in the moment meeting a need, we can experience it fully. Try it. Stop everything for a few minutes and experience one of your needs. For me, meeting my "people need" is just being with them—no thoughts, no judgments, and no wishes—nothing but totally being with them. Likewise, when I am meeting my "teaching need," I just teach. To make this perfectly clear, we are not letting go of the thing we want or need itself, but of the wanting or needing. These two are completely different activities. Being with the very thing we want or need is so satisfying when we are totally there.

As with all "letting go" exercises, feel free to label what you are letting go of before you let it go. This will make it much easier to release it.

Keeping a Journal to Help Us to Let Go

I begin my day by writing in my journal. Often it is within fifteen minutes of my waking up. I'm the only one who will ever read it and this sense of privacy gives me the freedom to write about anything.

The main reason I keep a journal is that it helps me to let go. Yes, even on good days, I still have things I need to release. One day I saw a lady in a store who looked like an actress and I couldn't stop wondering if she actually was. You would think that would be an easy one for me to drop, but my curiosity latched onto it and wouldn't let it go. The next morning, I wrote about the experience in my journal and after a few minutes it was out of my head.

Of course, on days when I have less pleasant experiences, I have even more reason to let them go. One evening I was at a party and was telling a story to the people I was standing with. When I finished the story, all but one of the people laughed and in an instant I felt disappointed. I didn't know I was so interested in making <u>everyone</u> laugh, but when I wrote about it in my journal the next morning, I was able to let it go.

I think we've all had countless experiences of carrying around the memory of an event or encounter that we could easily have dropped if we had just talked with someone about it or had written about it in our journal. Likewise, I think we've all had the experience of finally letting go of such experiences and the peace of mind that has followed.

If you have never kept a journal, or if you have and you are not presently keeping one, please consider keeping one now. Feel free to keep your journal in a notebook, on your computer, or even on your phone—whatever is comfortable for you. But just make sure it's private because in order to be honest in your journal, you have to write with complete freedom. In addition, promise yourself that you will never share your journal with anyone. You can talk to others about something you've written in your journal, but just don't read it to them. Finally, make sure that those around you who know you are keeping a journal also know that it is private.

Chapter 2

SEE THINGS AS THEY ARE,

NOT AS I WOULD HAVE THEM

A few years ago, I learned how to cut the dead branches out of the trees in my backyard. I used a handsaw for the smaller branches, a chain saw for the larger ones, and a telescopic chain saw to reach branches high up in the tree. I also climbed the ladder to cut several dead branches out of the top of one tree and I had to be really careful, but afterwards the tree looked great. Over time, all the trees in my backyard thrived from my pruning.

Soon afterwards, I began to see trees in my neighbors' yards that also needed pruning. Then I noticed that trees along the streets in town needed work and before long I was looking at trees along the interstate. The world needed me and I wanted to make every tree as beautiful as the ones in my back yard.

You know what's coming. Yes, my desire to prune every tree in sight robbed me of the ability to see the trees for what they were. Many of them were already beautiful and each and every tree had its own character. My neighbor's tree had a dead branch that stuck straight up like a flagpole. A tree on a street in town that had been pruned by the electric company looked as if it were raising its arms cheering for the home team. A third tree had a branch that looked like a tongue sticking out in defiance at everyone.

Wanting things to be a certain way is no doubt a strain of perfectionism. I don't usually see myself as a perfectionist, but the above examples are certainly eligible for this diagnosis and these are not the only ones in my life.

I am, at my very core, a teacher and as with all teachers, I want my students to do well. I want them to attend class, to enjoy learning, to discover things on their own, to apply the things I teach them to a broad spectrum of activities, and to carry my lessons with them into their adult lives to be productive and happy. While some students match my desire perfectly (pun intended), some do not. Freshmen who are away from home for the first time often struggle with being on their own. Some get caught up in their social lives and neglect their studies. Others who commute to school and hold jobs may have trouble balancing competing demands on their time. Sometimes athletes are conflicted about the benefits of good grades when they know there is a chance of their being drafted into a professional team even before they graduate. My desire for them to become successful students may be good for them and for me, but it can also blur my vision and prevent me from seeing them for who they are.

My desires are not the only things that blind me. My fears can also act like sunglasses in the middle of the night. Mark Twain once said, "Most of my troubles never happened." I know that's true not only for him and me, but for lots of other people as well. I worry about getting to the airport on time, yet in most instances I arrive hours before I board. I worry about a storm the weather forecaster predicted and the storm never hits. In fact, in some instances, the sun is not once behind a cloud for the whole day. I worry about losing someone's friendship, yet the other person is merely incredibly busy doing exactly what I would have him do if I were him.

The trick, of course, is for me to see through my projections, to actually pause and look at the images coming to my eyes and the sounds coming to my ears. With a little effort, I can push through the fog and what is before me is truly magical: the cricket that sounds like a lawnmower trying to start up with a worn-out spark plug, the cab in the middle of the city that slithers between buses and pedestrians as if it were greased, my loved ones who are talking about their day and are saying something slightly different from anything they have ever said before.

A driver who goes forty miles per hour in the passing lane irritates me. I want him to pull over so that I can pass. Conversely, the grocery store employee who walks down aisle after aisle until he finds the box of dates I'm looking for makes me feel special. Yet in both instances, my underlying desire is causing the reaction I have. I want to get to work quickly, just as I want to find what I'm looking for where I'm looking for it when I shop. On one level, I can label both as normal. On another level, however, I am so much better off if I release these desires and let them float off into the universe.

When I let go of my fears and desires, I not only get new and unique experiences, I also get rest and joy. Projecting fear and desire is exhausting. Letting go is refreshing. Not only have most of my troubles never happened, they are rarely as fearsome as I imagine them to be. My life really is manageable when I have a clear mind. I discover that the student who misses class after class really needs to be on his own and experience the consequence of failure if he is to grow up. I now know that trees whose lower branches have died need the sap and energy in their upper branches if they are to get the sunlight being blocked by other trees. Letting go allows me to rise above the petty and to see the larger picture.

Seeing things as they are does not mean that I sit by while a neighbor's child needs help finding his soccer ball. It does not mean that I travel at forty miles per hour on a super highway to take in the newly painted yellow stripes. I ask my neighbor's child where was the ball when he last kicked it. I pay attention to my driving and travel the speed limit. In all instances, I open my eyes to see what is before me.

When I am at peace with myself, that peace spreads to others. "If Don can work with a student who arrived in this country only three days ago with a very limited knowledge of English, so can I." "If Don can wait patiently for the commuter to pull over, so can I." "If Don can see that gnarled tree for what it is, so can I." We are all growing in the same direction and those of us who can see things as they are will help the rest of us by leading the way.

Please take a minute to open your eyes to whatever is before you. If you can, drop everything you're thinking about and just look. Also, feel free to listen to whatever sounds you hear or any other sensations. Try to do this for several minutes, each time letting go of any thoughts that come up. When you're finished, jot down what you saw and heard and if you like, share it with a friend.

Seeing as Pinot— An example of Seeing Something As It Was And Not As I Would Have Had It

One night I woke around 2:00 AM to go to the bathroom and get a drink of water. I fully expected to see my cat Pinot asleep on my massage chair in the green bedroom. If he had been there, I would have petted his head gently for a few seconds, he would have purred, and I would have felt so happy. To my surprise, he was not there, so I walked into the bathroom. There he was, sitting on a towel I had placed on the radiator. I could tell immediately from the way he was staring out the window that he was looking at something.

Instead of petting him or picking him up, I whispered, "What are you looking at?"

He did not move, he did not look up at me, and he did not purr. Instead, he very intensely stared out the window.

I hunched down so that my eyes were at the same level as his, trying to see what he was looking at. The streetlight on the phone pole in front of the house made the street well lit, but there was no one walking up or down the street nor could I see a cat that might be attracting Pinot's attention. Again, I tried to stare in the same direction that Pinot was starring and all of a sudden I saw it—a white plastic bag in the middle of the street that someone must have dropped out of a car or maybe a bag that a dog-walker from up the street had carried. I continued to stare with Pinot and a few seconds later the bag moved. *That's strange*, I thought. *There's no wind, so what could make that bag move?*

A second later it moved again, this time to the right, then back to the left.

"Oh my," I whispered.

It was not a bag, but a white rabbit with long white ears. Once again it moved right, then left. My face tingled. I had been living here thirty-six years and had never once seen a white rabbit anywhere, much less one on the street. Just then the rabbit hopped about thirty feet to the left, stopped, and looked around. Pinot's head moved to the left as did mine. The rabbit then turned away from us and hopped in a straight line across our neighbor's front lawn only to disappear around the side of his house.

I was amazed and stood up. Pinot kept starring out the window—perhaps thinking that the rabbit would return, so I followed his example and waited a few minutes starring in the same direction. When the rabbit did not return, I petted Pinot and left. As I said, for me it was a truly amazing experience.

I tell this story because if I had seen things as I would have had them, I would have picked Pinot up off the radiator and petted him. I would have missed seeing the rabbit and I would also have missed sharing this experience with my dear friend. Fortunately, that night I saw things as they were and not as I would have had them.

Please take a moment to recall a time when you saw something as it was and feel free to share this experience with a friend. In addition, spend a few moments seeing things as they are and if you like, add this to your journal.

Chapter 3

Help Things Become What They Were Meant To Be

When I was fourteen, I started a choir for the local Roman Catholic Church I attended. I had taken piano, violin, and trumpet lessons and knew enough about music to pull it off. The members of the choir were mostly ten to fourteen year old girls and boys and we sang the traditional hymns that were popular in the 1950s. I would stand with my back to the congregation and direct the choir and the organist. The choir sang about six to ten hymns throughout the service and after a while, we got good. Too good.

The pastor approached me one day and said we could no longer sing at Mass. We were disbanded. Why? Apparently, members of the congregation were paying more attention to the choir at the rear of the church than the service in the front of the church and some parishioners were coming to the 10:00 o'clock Mass just to hear the choir. That was just too much for the pastor. I felt disappointed, but I pretty much took it in stride. After all, I was not the pastor, it was not "my" church, and I was only fourteen.

Today, I look back on this incident with much different eyes.

What I see is a group of youngsters who love to sing, who have a certain amount of devotion and loyalty to their church, and who are good enough to entertain others. Knowing what I know now, if I were the pastor, I would have encouraged the continued development of the choir. I would have scheduled times in addition to Mass for the choir to perform and if at all possible, I would have entered the choir into a competition so that it would bring attention to my church. Most of all, I would see these youngsters as good people who were headed in a positive direction—and I would do everything I could to help them get there.

My pastor's view of the world was pretty much the view held by most other people at that time. Students were to follow the rules, regardless. Of all my teachers throughout elementary and high school, I'm sure many saw our potential but I can recall only three who helped us become what we were meant to be—my fourth grade French teacher, my high-school band director, and my twelfth grade English teacher.

My French teacher believed we could learn French. She spoke French to us, treated us with enormous respect and enthusiasm, and made learning fun and exciting. Unfortunately, her fiancé was killed in an auto accident and she left us after one year.

When I entered ninth grade, we got a new band director and at our first practice he had us play a piece. I recall his directing us for all of thirty seconds before he doubled over with laughter. Yes, we were that bad. He stopped band practice altogether and spent about a month teaching us individually how to play our instruments. He worked our butts off—and when we came back together as a band, we were so much better. Yes, it made a difference that he came to us after a career playing trumpet on Broadway in New York City and yes, it made a difference that he knew every single instrument, but most of all, he believed in us.

My twelfth grade English teacher did not have an engaging personality, but she did help us to see where we could take our academic writing. I recall her coming up beside me one day as we were working at our desks she said to me, "Make your opening stronger." As she said that, she looked at me with a stern face and held up her fist. I did what she told me to do and the piece improved.

Being surrounded by top educators in my professional life has made a huge difference for me and four in particular strengthened my habit of helping things become what they were meant to be. Jim Gray, Founder of the National Writing Project, believed in celebrating teachers and good teaching and he made teachers the core of staff development. I recall one afternoon as he was driving me from UC Berkeley to the Oakland airport. We had had several discussions about his approach which placed teachers at the center of education and I think he sensed my difficulty grasping it. Yes, he had to spell it out for me, but once he did, I got it.

Donald Graves was an expert on teaching writing to elementary students. I had been a compassionate parent to my three children, but I learned from Don what it meant to really listen to them. Compartmentalized thinking had kept me from transferring what I had learned from archery and living in the woods to raising children, but once I saw the connection, the transformation was major and lasting. Consequently, while other parents struggled with their teenagers, I listened to mine and fell in love with them.

Don Murray, writing teacher and journalist from the University of New Hampshire, was the first person I had ever seen turn his back on the class. It was during the 1978 NVWP Summer Institute when he wrote on the board a very personal piece about losing his daughter at the age of twenty in an automobile accident. He knew we were trying to become writers and by showing us how he wrote, he led the way.

And finally, Jim Moffett, scholar and meditator, helped us to connect our inner selves to our writing and teaching. In his article, "Writing, Inner Speech, and Meditation," he connected all three at a time when educators were not allowed to use the term meditation in the classroom, nor were they encouraged to have their students use their real thoughts in their writing.

To be honest, I have no idea where I got my propensity for helping people move in the direction in which they are growing. Perhaps I was born with it or maybe it came from my spending countless hours in the woods watching plants and animals grow. Whatever its origin, this way of thinking is at the very core of my being.

Frequently, I watch one of our cats come into our living room and head toward the sofa to scratch it. I know their scratching has something to do with greeting us and I can see that it is just part of their nature. So I simply say, "No, not the sofa," and bring them to the scratching post that stands at the entrance to the room. They scratch the post and look up at me as if to say, "Okay. It's not as much fun as the sofa, but it will do."

I see similar behavior in children who clamor for their parents' attention by interrupting a conversation. Some parents yell at their children, "Go away, we're talking," while others wrap their arms around them, lift them onto their laps, hug them, and whisper, "We'll be finished in a minute and then we can talk." Such children are so delighted to be hugged that they listen contentedly until the adults are finished.

I think my basic premise here is that we are all growing and evolving and that we are all waiting to take the next step in our evolution. A plant grows toward the sun, a child grows in her ability to communicate, and an adult grows in wisdom. My role in my own life, and in the lives of others, is to help us all become aware of the direction we are heading, figure out the next step, and then to help us to move in that direction.

At times we all know where we want to go, but we also make mistakes in the way we proceed. The employee who wants to get home quickly to see his loved one is better off calling ahead and expressing his love rather than racing ninety miles per hour on the interstate. The mother who is irritated with a pestering child is better off taking a few minutes from her busy routine to pay attention to him rather than screaming, "Go away!" The nation that is struggling with crime is better off helping people to get jobs than placing them in prison.

Psychologists call this Applied Behavioral Analysis Therapy and both teachers and therapists use this with autistic children to find alternative and appropriate behaviors to replace inappropriate behaviors. As my friend Kelly Worland, an elementary teacher, once said, "If we identify and nurture potential, then we can give people what they need to be who they truly are."

Modeling is a similar strategy used by therapists, teachers, and leaders who know the ripple effect of saying and doing things that will help others to get what they need in order to grow. When one person in a relationship says, "Thank you," and the second replies, "Whatever," the first can then say, "You're so welcome and thank you for thanking me." The rephrasing may be startling at first, but after a while it can become second nature.

The peace and happiness that comes from our all helping each other in acts small and large makes this well worth our time.

Many years ago, Betty Edwards wrote an article that has become a central part of the way I teach writing. The title of the article is "Madman, Architect, Carpenter, Judge," and these four roles are crucial in writing. If you start your piece acting like a madman, you'll get your ideas down, but if you start your piece acting like a judge, you'll create writer's block and will not be able to write at all. After the madman comes the architect, the one who designs the draft, followed by the carpenter—the one who builds the draft part by part. Finally, the judge is necessary to look back on the draft and decide what works and what doesn't. So, all four roles are necessary in order to produce a draft, but the writer has to know when to use each one.

These four roles can also be applied to life. If you're constantly acting the role of a madman but never stepping back to allow the architect, carpenter, or judge to do their parts, your life and relationships will be chaos. Similarly, if you have an overactive judge, you will stifle creativity.

Our friends Carol and Ken went to dinner with us one evening. Ken said judgmental things and Carol said madman things—and the result was that they were not happy with each other. Carol responded to Ken's criticism by rolling her eyes and saying "Whatever," while Ken criticized virtually everything Carol said. It was part of Carol's personality to blurt things out, often talking without thinking, as if her inner speech was her outer speech. And it was Ken's personality as a very intellectual and bright professional to constantly say, "That's not true," or "That's not possible." The result was that they stifled rather than supported each other's ideas.

As I listened to them, I thought, *They need to see things as they are so that they can help each other become what they were meant to be.* I knew that the first step each one needed was to be listened to by the other. If I had thought of it at the time, I would have told them about Betty Edward's article and would have said, "Ken, Carol is being a 'madman,' so just listen to her talk like a madman. Just listen." And likewise, I would have said to Carol, "Carol, Ken is being a judge, so just listen to him talk like a judge." I'm sure this listening would have opened up a whole world of appreciation for both of them.

As it turned out, Ken sat in the front seat next to me as I drove us back from the restaurant and, in part because I listened to him, we had a wonderful conversation. Both Ken and I played the judge, both of us being critical of an event we had heard in the news, and we both felt free to say whatever we wanted because we knew the other would hear us. At the same time, my wife Ceres was having a wonderful conversation with Carol in the back seat, both of them being madmen, both talking on and on and enjoying the freedom of being themselves.

Some mornings I'll be in the kitchen making salad for lunch, emptying the dishwasher, and listening to the news on the radio. I'll be in my architect/carpenter mode as I plan my day. Suddenly, Ceres will come into the kitchen in her judge mode and criticize the actions of someone in the news. Upon hearing her, my first thought is, *Hush. Don't pollute the news. Just take it in.* Then my next thought is, *Look out. She's in judge mode.* Once I reach that step, I say, "Yeah, calling 911 while he was robbing a bank wasn't smart." Ceres then feels listened to and we soon begin to listen to each other.

We are all trying to take the next step. Our pets nuzzle up to us so that they can be pet, plants stretch around each other so they can get sunlight, and even cars "complain" when they need a checkup. Ironically, sometimes we have the hardest time seeing our own next steps, but having others around us who listen to us can be a big help. We then see ourselves as we are and that in itself points us in the direction of seeing what our next steps are.

When I was a sophomore in college, I and a number of my classmates were sitting outside and enjoying the warm, spring afternoon. The conversation drifted in the direction of what careers we saw ourselves entering. Even though I was part of the conversation, I had no idea what I would do. Suddenly, one of my classmates pointed at me and said, "You're going to be a teacher." I was shocked. Never once had I thought of becoming a teacher and at first it made no sense. In fact, it took me several weeks before I agreed with him. If he hadn't "listened" to me (by the way, I was totally unaware he had even noticed me at all during our freshman and sophomore years), he could not have helped me to take the next step that was to go for a Ph.D. in English so that I could teach on the college level.

If you like, please take a few minutes to jot down a several experiences you've had with helping people and/or things become what they were meant to be. As I did in this chapter, please include stories of times you've helped others and times when others have helped you. If you have a desire to help someone but you have not yet had a chance to do so, feel free to add this to your "to do" list.

Where Do We Belong?

I first came up with this question when I was teaching a class in which one student was writing a piece in which she was trying to make up her mind whether or not she should stay in the United States or move to Crete after she graduated from college. Her parents had come from Crete and she wasn't making any real progress in choosing one over the other.

At the time, I was expanding my practice of meditation by reading books on Zen and I found that the koans, or puzzles as some people call them, helped me to shift my thinking from rational, judgmental thinking to holistic thinking. When I first came upon the famous koan "What is the sound of one hand clapping?" I was befuddled. As everyone knows, we need two hands to clap, not one. The more I worked with the question, the more my rational mind gave up arguing with it and the more my holistic mind accepted the peace that became the answer for me. The sound of one hand clapping is a very quiet mind.

When I held a mini-conference with my student, I asked her, "Where do you belong?"

She became silent and I could see her having the same reaction to my question that I had to the koans I was studying. She said, "I don't know, but I'll think about it."

When she handed in the next draft of her paper the following week, she thanked me for asking the question and told me she had decided that she considered herself an American and that it didn't matter where she lived.

Little did I know at the time that the question I asked her was a question I would ask other people who were also trying to make such decisions, including a colleague who was trying to decide whether she should stay at Mason and pursue another advanced degree or teach at another university. As it turned out, she decided to pursue an advanced degree and stay at Mason. I also asked this question of a friend who was divorced and looking for a new partner. She is now much more focused in her dating.

Once you think about the functions of our two ways of thinking, all this makes sense. Our rational mind uses reason, and often argues about one point after the other. Our holistic mind, however, bundles everything together and comes up with a decision. In addition, I've found that with practice I can use my holistic mind to make even relatively small daily decisions. I use the "Where do I belong?" question frequently to decide what I should do on a given day, especially when it appears to be a toss-up between two relatively similar tasks. This holistic approach pulls in factors I would never think of when I use only my rational mind and the end result is that I'm much more at peace with myself.

Feel free to take a moment to ask yourself the question "Where do I belong?" and see what happens. Allow for a period of quiet as your mind shifts from rational thinking to holistic thinking. Also feel free to make up a holistic question on your own, one that on the surface makes no sense and proves frustrating to the rational mind. Again, after you ask yourself your holistic question, allow for a brief period of silence while the mind shifts from rational to holistic. When the answer comes, you can tell it's from the holistic side because it usually comes suddenly as one whole answer. It might even come as an image or a feeling. Give yourself a moment to be with your answer because I think you'll find that moment filled with peace.

Chapter 4

MEDITATION

I'll get to the connection between meditation and a peaceful life in a minute, but let me start by telling you how I got into meditation in the first place.

When I was thirty and had been teaching at George Mason University for five years, my office mate—Bob Karlson—came in one Monday morning and said to me, "Sit down, Gallehr. I'm going to teach you how to meditate."

I later learned that he had just come back from a weekend where he learned Transcendental Meditation and he was eager to share his experiences with me. His instructions were simple: sit in a chair with your back straight and head titled slightly forward, eyes almost closed, feet flat on the floor, hands cupped and resting in one another in your lap, and repeat a mantra for twenty minutes.

"Do that twice a day," he said.

Because I liked the restfulness I experienced from meditating and because I was a little intimidated by my 6'5" deep-voiced office mate, I meditated twice a day from that day forward.

Unlike Bob, I never took a class in Transcendental Meditation, nor did I ever join a meditation group. In the early 1980s, however, I

did start reading books on meditation—namely Janwillem van de We-
tering's *A Glimpse of Nothingness* and *The Empty Mirror.* Van de We-
tering was a Dutch fiction writer who had left Holland in his early
twenties searching for the meaning of life after the horrors of WWII.
He traveled to Africa, then up along South America in the Pacific only
to end up knocking on the door of a Zen monastery in Kyoto, Japan.
I loved his books—in part because they were well written and in part
because I liked the peace they gave me. For about ten years, I read
them over and over every night before falling asleep. One of the high-
lights of my life was meeting Janwillem and having him sign one of
his books.

When he held it in his hand and looked at it, he said, "Well worn."

I was shy and all I could say was, "I read it over and over."

By the mid-1980s my life had changed because of meditation.
People described me as calm and my actions as thoughtful. I was
more considerate of people—in other words I didn't have to apologize for being rude or stupid. I was also able to concentrate better
by letting distractions slip by. When I taught, I saw difficulties my
students were experiencing such as fear of rejection or writer's
block as passing events and I showed them how to be patient, recognize the feelings they were having as normal, and how to let go
of them.

As I mentioned above, when I meditate I sit in an upright chair,
place my feet on the floor, tilt my pelvis slightly forward so that my
spine is resting on itself, tilt my head slightly down so that I am looking at the floor in a forty-five degree angle, place my hands cupped
together in my lap, and I usually close my eyes.

I then follow a three-step process. During the first five to ten minutes of my meditation, I watch my thoughts as they rise, label each
one, and let them go. For instance, the following thought popped up
one day as I began my meditation: *I don't know how to respond to Mark's*

email, but I do want him to see me as wise and intelligent. I then labeled it one of those "I want people to like me" thoughts and let it go. What followed was a brief moment of silence, peace, and detachment. When I got to work, I figured out how to respond to Mark's email without all the mental interference.

In the second part of my meditation, I use a mantra. Mantras are sounds or sayings that are intended to create a spiritual transformation or to protect the mind, and they came originally from the Vedic tradition in India before spreading to Hinduism, Buddhism, and other Eastern traditions. The traditional mantras I use range from the word "Om" or "Aum" that some people consider the sound of supreme consciousness to "Om Mani Padme Hum" which means the jewel in the lotus. I also use "Om shanti, shanti, shanti" which means "peace, peace, peace permeating the whole universe". Om basically means the entire universe is moving. Sometimes I use these during my full twenty-minute meditation, but mostly I use them in the middle in order to calm my mind.

In the third part of my meditation, usually the last five to ten minutes, I just sit and let go of both thoughts and mantras. Yes, they come back from time to time, but despite that these are moments when my discursive mind is quiet and I am at peace.

The first part of this three-step meditation—the watch, label, and let go—has also become a habit in the rest of my day. Not every single moment of my life, but most moments—enough that this way of living is now who I am. In fact, whenever I am having a problem, this way of thinking helps me to avoid knee-jerk reactions and reminds me to pause. It can be something as simple as not eating a second candy bar to helping someone who is totally out of control. The end result for me is a life worth living.

Now, to answer a few questions that people usually have about meditation.

Does one really need to meditate for twenty minutes twice a day? The research on meditation tells us that if we are to get the benefits that come from meditating, we need to sit for twenty minutes. It's like an athlete exercising for only an hour a week—it just isn't enough. By the way, both brain research and meditation traditions support the idea of meditating for twenty minutes twice a day. I'll explain this in detail later in this chapter.

What if you're very busy and can't find the time to sit? This is one I have struggled with for years and the way I approach it is through numbers. On days when I don't meditate, I am a lot less focused, I interrupt myself, and I waste time. Several years ago I actually jotted down the amount of time I wasted in a given day—and it always came to more than forty minutes. The other way I justify taking the time to meditate is in the quality of my life. Without meditation, I'm not the nicest guy on the planet, nor the wisest. I can be rude, thoughtless, and stupid. The time I spend apologizing for my inconsiderate actions and trying to make up for them can far outstrip the time I would have spent meditating. This said, on days I can't sit twice, I sit once and that's so much better than not sitting at all.

What if you feel all alone in your meditating? There are times when I do because I really like people and love being with them. So, I have a friend whom I call my Meditation Buddy. She occasionally meditates with me in person, sometimes at the same time I do but in a different location, but most often we meditate at different times and in different places. Nevertheless, I still consider her "with me" each time I meditate. For me, that's a big help.

What about books to read on meditation? There are lots of books out there and lots of websites. What works for me is to read a book on meditation at bedtime because it not only helps me to relax and fall asleep, but it also helps me feel connected to the larger population of people who meditate. Forming a meditation group serves a similar purpose and the group can even agree to read and discuss the same books.

Where do exercise and journaling fit in with meditation? Writing for about five to ten minutes in my journal before I meditate lets me get things off my chest, just as working out gets the crud out of my body. In fact, for me they work together and I often do both before sitting. You can figure out what is the best routine for you, but make sure that these three activities (meditating, journaling, and exercising) work together and support each other.

What if you just don't have the time on a given day to spend twenty minutes meditating? Then meditate for ten minutes, or five, or one. Or meditate for one minute between activities during the day. Don't get caught up on an all or nothing way of thinking. Do the best you can and that will be enough.

Deciding to Meditate

Sometime in the 1970s, my late wife and I went to a Marriage Encounter workshop and one of the things we were told was, "Love is a decision." At the time it made no sense to me. Love was something you felt and either you felt love toward someone or you didn't.

It took years before I accepted this as a possibility and years more before I made it my practice. Perhaps the defining moment came when I imagined the consequences of my actions. If I decide to love someone, the consequences are a continued relationship that over time means a great deal to me. If I decide not to love this person, the loss of the relationship also means a great deal to me and I am not willing to sacrifice the subsequent losses that are sure to follow.

Now it is a habit for me to make love a decision. If a friend is being a real pain in the butt, I return love because I want to continue the friendship, go out to dinner, and have good times together. Treating love as a decision also shifts me into long-term thinking and away from impulse actions. I'm a lot wiser in my head than I am in my emotional reactions and I love the life that my wisdom provides me.

I have learned, also over time, to use the same process when I meditate. I have plenty of moments when I don't feel like meditating, moments when I want to read a book, take a walk, or listen to the news. Needless to say, like everyone else, I have an incredibly busy life. Lots of people in Northern Virginia commute to work despite the days when we're able to telecommute. We also have friends and family who deserve if not require our time and attention. Then there's yard work, school, cooking meals, doing laundry, reading a book to the children, on and on it goes....

I wish I could say I sit the same time every morning, but it doesn't work that way for me. Despite my day planner and everything else that sets out my day for me, there is the unexpected. The cat has escaped into the basement and it takes ten minutes to lure her up with promises of "Turkey, turkey—come on—here's turkey for you." Or the child who has come down with a cold and has crawled into bed only to cough and cough and cough. Or the unexpected rainfall that makes it necessary to leave a half hour earlier than usual to make it to work on time. Yes, some days it is just not possible to chisel out twenty minutes to sit, but most days it is.

One other thought about deciding to meditate. No one is one hundred percent wise. We all do foolish or stupid things. But in looking back over any given day, most of us want to be proud of the decisions we've made. Yes, some decisions we wish we didn't have to make, but given that, we have choices and making decisions that bring out the best in us are well worth making. With them made, our lives are simpler, wiser, and more compassionate and as far as I'm concerned, this is as good as it gets.

Please take a moment to jot down any thoughts you may have about your making a decision to meditate, then take a look at what tomorrow looks like and see if you can schedule a twenty-minute meditation. If placing "meditate" in your day planner helps, please do so.

Using Mini-meditations During The Day

Most of the people I associate with, students, colleagues, friends, and even neighbors, are very busy people. It is not at all unusual for them to put in twelve to sixteen-hour days studying, working, taking care of children, doing yard work, etc. Some of my colleagues come to a weekly meditation session, but like me, they have days when they just don't have the time to sit. I can on most days, but sometimes my day begins at 6:00 in the morning and doesn't end until midnight.

Even on busy days however, there are usually moments when I don't have anything I have to do. Sometimes I'll get to a meeting early or I'll finish reading student papers and have a minute before I have to answer texts or emails. In addition, because I like to be on time and my wife doesn't mind being late, I am usually ready to leave about ten minutes before she is, so I'll sit on a chair by the front door and just breathe—inhale and exhale. Sometimes I get as much as five or ten minutes to do a mini-meditation and it is so refreshing. I feel as if I have been given a chance to open my eyes. I actually see the furniture in the hall, the leaves on the trees outside, and of course my beloved cat Pinot stretching out on the floor. Another time of the day that I do a mini-meditation is during the night when I wake up after sleeping for about four hours. Rather than check email, surf the web, or read the newspaper, I lie in bed and relax, paying attention to my breathing, noticing my thoughts as they come and as they go. By doing this I find that I go back to sleep much more quickly and sleep much more soundly.

In addition to opening my eyes and helping me to relax, these mini-meditations give me is a deeper meditation when I get a chance to sit for twenty minutes. We all know that the more stressed we are, the longer the early part of the meditation is—the part when thoughts are racing through our heads. By letting go of thoughts periodically throughout the day and night, I am able to meditate much more deeply when I sit for twenty minutes.

Finally, mini-meditations increase my ability to listen to others. Rather than my having a knee-jerk reaction, I hear both the surface meaning of what they are saying and the deeper meaning. A student who sends me an email apologizing because she didn't get all her homework done is also telling me that she wishes she had more time and wishes that she could do the work she really wants to do. My response then is filled with understanding: "I'm sorry you didn't get a chance to finish your piece this week. I understand it's mid-terms for your other four classes. I hope you get a chance to catch up next week."

Please consider doing a few mini-meditations when you have a chance during the day. I think you'll find they bring the same benefits to you that they bring to me.

Other Mantras

Here I am going to talk not about traditional mantras, but about mantras I create myself.

I think all of us from time to time have days that are filled with "undesirable" tasks, ones that either do not give us energy or ones that take energy away and for each of us, they're different. For me, on days when I have to do budgets or when I have to do my taxes, I come away looking for something that will restore my spirit. Even worse are days when I have to deal with the effects of budget cuts—days when I have to explain to someone that his or her job is no longer funded. These days are not just a drain on me, they are very, very, sad.

Like most people, I try to find something positive when I have an undesirable task—such as the fact that my tax money will support a public school teacher, a policeman, and a fireman. I can't imagine my life without these people and putting up with a day of placing numbers on a tax form is a small price to pay. If I have to tell a student he is no longer passing my course, I make sure I also tell him that he will benefit greatly from taking it over because he will then enter the workplace prepared to make a good salary.

In addition to my finding the positive side of undesirable tasks, I also try to come up with a mini-mantra that I can use as I'm working. I repeat the first part of the mantra while inhaling and the second part while exhaling. For instance, I'll inhale with the words, "I am," and exhale with the word, "happy." Another one I use is, "I am…peace" and a third is "I am…silly." This last one makes me giggle.

Another way I create a mini-mantra is by adding a person's name after the "I am….". For instance, one of my friends is an excellent math teacher, so when I have to work on a budget I say to myself, "I am…Laura." Sometimes when I have to wait for a long line of traffic to move, I'll say, "I am…Buddha" and I picture the little pot-bellied statue of Buddha one of my students gave me as a gift. Then when I'm in a meeting that has become unusually contentious, I'll say "I am…Jesus" and recall the many things Jesus did to bring peace and love to the tribes in Israel.

How do I use these mini-mantras when I meditate? As I said earlier, I usually use them in the middle—after using the "label and let go" exercise and before just sitting. Can my using these mini-mantras during the day replace my twenty-minute meditation sessions? No. The depth is just not there with a mini-mantra when I am also dealing with the complexity of daily life. However, the effect of reciting these mini-mantras is much greater than you would expect. First of all, they give me enough distance from the undesirable tasks to enable me to let go of the tension that I've built up. Second, they change my breathing from short to long. And third, they restore my sense of humor.

I encourage you to create a range of mantras and feel free to select ones that you really like because they work for you. Again, feel free to share these with your meditation buddy.

Meditation and Brain Research

Several years after I began meditating, Vic Kryston, one of my friends, gave me a button that read, "Oh, Go Meditate!" I laughed. We both knew that when we meditated on a regular basis, others knew as well. We were kinder, more focused, more productive, and in our field— better writers and better teachers.

When I first used meditation in my classes, I didn't use the word "meditation," but instead told my students that we were going to use a technique that Phil Jackson taught his Chicago Bulls basketball players (1989-1998). Why didn't I use the word meditation in class? Meditation in those days was associated with religion and I didn't want to alarm my students by thinking I was introducing religion into a writing class. Of course, some of my students made the connection but many of them adopted meditation as part of their writing process. As far as I could tell, it eliminated writer's block, improved their ability to give and receive feedback, and helped them produce better pieces because they were able to stay focused throughout long hours of revision.

Much has changed since the 1980s and today people from all walks of life use meditation. Why? I think the two things that have most secularized meditation are the widespread practice of yoga and brain research. Books such as *Zen and the Brain* by James H. Austin and *Brain Literacy for Educators and Psychologists* by Virginia W. Berninger and Todd L. Richards bridge several fields at once. Professional journals now publish articles on this topic on a regular basis, including "Mindfulness {ractice leads to increases in regional brain gray matter density," that was published in *Psychiatry Research* in January 2011. The meditation technique used in this study they called Mindfulness-Based Stress Reduction (MBSR). The results from the group of sixteen people who were not previously meditators but who went through an eight-week MBSR program, was that at the end of the study they, compared to the control group, had more gray matter in the portion of their brains that was "...involved in learning and memory processes, emotion regulation, self-referential processing, and perspective taking." More specifically, there was more gray matter in the hippocampus where learning and memory are located and less in the amygdala, the section that houses anxiety and stress.

I find this and even more recent studies to be fascinating for two reasons. Not only do they confirm what I've experienced in my own practice and what I've seen in friends and students who meditate, but when I look at the brain scans in these studies, there is no denying that these people's brains before and after the study are radically different.

As I mentioned earlier, I became a meditator because my office mate told me to meditate. Would I have become a meditator if I had only read an article about meditation increasing gray matter? Probably not. Would I have become a meditator if my friends were and I noticed a beneficial change in them, changes that I admired? I think I would have given it a shot.

If you already meditate, feel free to read a few meditation/brain research studies just to broaden your understanding of what's going on inside your head. If you don't, and you think reading about these studies might change your mind, please do. In addition, feel free to ask your meditation buddy if he or she would like to read an article or two about meditation and brain research. Sharing this information with your buddy will be really enjoyable.

Chapter 5

NOTHING IS STRONGER
THAN THE DESIRE TO FEEL COMFORTABLE

We've all heard of the phrase "nature versus nurture" and in the first section of this chapter I'll focus on nurture—the things we carry with us from childhood, things that were created by how we were raised, by the many experiences we had in school, and by our friends.

Allow me to begin by telling you how I became aware that how I was raised was strongly influencing my life as an adult.

In 1979, I went to an Ira Progoff Intensive Journal Workshop and thereafter kept a journal for one year. In 1980, I reread my journal and became so depressed that I stopped keeping it for a whole month. What depressed me was seeing myself make the same mistakes over and over. What mistakes were I making? For one, I wanted to please people and consequently I was saying "yes" to requests at times when I should have said "no". The fallout was that I had too many things on my calendar and didn't have enough time to do things well. Another mistake I was making was allowing a conversation or discussion to end on a negative note. Why was I making this mistake? I had had so many conversations in my childhood end on a negative note that I had become used to them and wanted to repeat this feeling. A third mistake I was making came from my growing up allowing what we now call "control freaks" to run the show. If they were insistent, I gave in and usually walked away unhappy. Such behavior was not good for me, nor was it good for the "control freak".

When I returned to my journal, I was determined to change the way I lived. I had no problems with making mistakes—I just didn't want to make the same ones over and over. I wanted to learn from my mistakes and move on.

One change I made was that I began to approach "control freaks" with a plan of action, such as being prepared to say, "I feel really uncomfortable with the direction this meeting is going." The first time I did this, I was very surprised that the other people listened to me and even more surprised that we all were able to change the direction of the discussion.

Another example of doing something that initially made me uncomfortable was doing the research necessary to make an informed decision. You would think that someone who taught research procedures as part of his job would do research when preparing to cast a vote, make a purchase, or paint a fence. Compartmentalized thinking being what it is, many of the things I did in my personal life I did out of habit. I was not at all comfortable reading about a matter that was coming before Congress and then writing a letter to my congressman telling him what I thought. It wasn't a big deal, but it took guts for me to do it. Needless to say, I was totally surprised when I received a four-page letter from my congressman thanking me for my letter and setting out in detail his current thinking on the subject.

Making a significant change in our lives often makes us uncomfortable. We get used to the situations and emotions that have formed our lives and even when we know in our heads and our hearts that a particular sequence is unhealthy, we continue the pattern because it is comfortable. It is what we know. The desire to feel comfortable impacts all parts of our lives—from decisions on where to live, who to live with, and what occupation to choose. We may joke about choosing a mate who is exactly like one of our parents, but it is often true. If our parents have given us a loving, supportive environment in which to grow up, that's fine. Unfortunately, if our parents are mean to us, we tend to surround ourselves with people who treat us poorly and in order to change things we may have to go through a stage in which we are very uncomfortable because we're hanging out with really nice people. Again, the trick is to recognize these uncomfortable feelings, label them, and let them go.

Routine switching is hard for all of us. When I make such a change, I have to write about it in my journal, create a plan of action, and enlist the help of others to support me. After my 1980 journal epiphany, I began to make decisions based on what was best for me, for my loved ones, and for the world I inhabited. One thing I changed, as I mentioned in the previous chapter, was how I began each day: I wrote in my journal (five to ten minutes), exercised (five to ten minutes), and meditated (twenty minutes). To establish this habit and to become comfortable with it, I initially required support. I read books and articles on all three so that I felt as if I were part of a community. I talked to people about what I was doing and this prompted them to ask me about it the next time they saw me. And I kept in mind the benefits of this practice—better mental and physical health, a sense of equanimity, and a plan of action for the day.

It is best that when we become aware of our uncomfortable feelings, we recognize them, and let them go. The actions we then take have a much better chance of helping us to become the person we were meant to be.

Please take a minute to jot down some of the things you do that are based on how you were raised. If you're happy with any of them, keep them. If you're not, see if you can lay out a plan of action to change what you're doing.

Being Aware Of Our Basic Nature

In this section I will focus on the things we carry with us that come from our basic nature—the very nature we had when we came into this world. If you're like me, some parts of your nature you may really like, while other parts you wish you could leave in a dumpster. Regardless, over time we identify with these traits and find ourselves saying such things as "This is just who I am."

Before examining where these nature traits may have come from, I want to say that the importance of knowing these traits is that by doing so we can make decisions much more clearly, and eventually we will bring peace to ourselves. If we are constantly befuddled about why we're comfortable or uncomfortable in a certain situation, we will have a much harder time acting in a way that is in our long-term best interests.

There are several theories about the origins of our basic nature and I would like to start with genes. There is no denying that many of us look like our parents—either like our mom, our dad, or a mixture of both. My first son looks and acts like me while my second son looks and acts like my late wife Diana. My daughter is definitely a mixture of both of us—Diana's height and my color. As parents, most of us so see how genes can cause our basic nature that we often joke about where a son or daughter came from if he or she acts differently from us.

Before going further, I want to give you a heads up that I will be entering a few areas that some of you may feel uncomfortable with and if that's the case, that's fine. Just skip to the next section. There are lots of ways that people come to know their basic nature and I have no preference for the particular way you choose. In the end, I want you to be able to say, "I am feeling comfortable (or uncomfortable) in this situation because of my basic nature."

In addition to genes, astrological signs are another way we can explain our basic nature. Yes, many of us were skeptical when we first learned that the time of year in which we were born could make us one kind of person or another, but it goes beyond reason when we notice that our Virgo friends really like to work and that our Gemini friends are really fun to be around because they seem to have more than one personality. At the very least, it is worth knowing our astrological signs in case they shed light on a basic trait that we have that can't be explained by genes. I'm a Scorpio. Two of the negative qualities of Scorpios are vengeance and discord and I have to admit that I have negative thoughts from time to time and I have no idea where they come from. They certainly don't come from my genes or my upbringing. In addition, I've seen these traits in other Scorpios and neither genes nor upbringing explain them. Similarly, the Libras I know constantly see both sides of any issue and consequently they have trouble making decisions. "It could be this…then again, it could be that." There are countless ways to access your astrological signs, but just in case you haven't seen this, here's a basic chart.

Sign	Major Trait	Positive Characteristics	Negative Ones
ARIES	self	courage, initiative, pioneer instinct	brash rudeness, selfish impetuosity
TAURUS	money	endurance, loyalty, wealth	obstinacy, gluttony
GEMINI	mind	versatility	capriciousness, unreliability
CANCER	family	sympathy, homing instinct	clannishness, childishness
LEO	children	love, authority, integrity	egotism, force
VIRGO	work	purity, industry, analysis	fault-finding, cynicism
LIBRA	marriage	harmony, justice	vacillation, superficiality
SCORPIO	sex	survival, regeneration	vengeance, discord
SAGITTARIUS	travel	optimism, higher learning	lawlessness
CAPRICORN	career	depth	narrowness, gloom
AQUARIUS	friends	human fellowship, genius	perverse unpredictability
PISCES	confinement	spiritual love universality	diffusion, escapism

Again, my point here is not to prove or disprove astrology, but to use it in case it can help us to identify an aspect of our basic nature. If you are interested in studying astrology further, there are countless books and websites. There are even people who will read your astrological

signs for you and give you a much more detailed list than I've pro-
vided above.

A third way to explain our basic nature is to look at the possibility
that we may have been here before and we may even be traveling with
the same people from one life to another. I have to admit that if I
should get a chance to come back to this world in the future, I would
love to be with the people who surround me now.

Allow me to tell you of an experience I had in 2002. I was standing
looking at my wife Ceres and all of a sudden I was recalling a time in
the 1800s when I was an artist in Paris and was doing a portrait of her.
She was from the royal class, I was not, and for some reason she was giving me a hard time because she didn't want to sit still. It's the only experience I've had like it, but it felt so real that I totally believe it actually
happened. Somewhat ironically, when I enrolled in an art class when I
was in my early twenties, I copied a portrait done by the Dutch portrait
painter Frans Hals and when in my forties I enrolled in a photography
class, I found myself taking pictures of people. There is nothing in my
genes or my upbringing that explains why I love to do portraits and while
I have no way of proving that I was a portrait artist in the 1800s, if a psychic were to say I was, I would reply, "That makes sense."

Years ago one of my friends, Jim Moffett, said that there were re-
cordings of young people talking to each other about what it was like
on the other side. I was surprised. Several years later I read a book
edited by Blair Underwood called *Before I Got Here: The Wondrous
Things We Hear When We Listen to the Souls of Our Children* and learned
that there is a whole field of study called reincarnation research and
past life regression. In addition I came across the work of Ian Steven-
son, a Canadian biochemist and professor of psychiatry at the University of Virginia, who conducted more than 2,500 studies of young
children who said they remembered events that occurred during a
previous life.

From my perspective, such things explain how we come to have the basic nature that we do, a nature that makes us comfortable with one thing and not comfortable with another. Just as I'm comfortable doing portraits, for instance, I would be bored out of my skull if I had to do landscapes.

Why is this important? As I said earlier, I don't think anything is stronger than the desire to feel comfortable and if we're experiencing a particular feeling, it is so much easier to make smart decisions if we know what is causing the feeling.

I had a student once who was very bright and an excellent writer. Halfway through my course, she wrote a piece about how her mother had just told her, "You're going to law school to become a lawyer." In effect, her mother was giving her an order and she was to obey it. My student came from a culture in which it was not that unusual for parents to select a spouse for their child and consequently my student planned to become a lawyer. It was not my job to interfere, but I did tell my student, as I have told others who had similar abilities in writing, that it would be wonderful if she found a way to keep writing after she graduated from college—either in a job or as a hobby. I didn't know her childhood that well, but from what I could see, her being a writer was coming from her basic nature. About six months later, I got an email from her saying that after studying for the LSAT she decided not to go to law school. I could tell from her email that she was very happy with the way things had turned out.

Choosing a career is one of the most important decisions we make—as is choosing a spouse or partner, a lifestyle, and a location in which to live. In addition to these large decisions, we are also faced with countless smaller ones, some of which are really difficult. That's okay. When it comes to small decisions, life allows for us to go in one direction or another without dire consequences and then life also gives us a second chance and a third…

Please take a moment to jot down some of the things that you consider to be part of your basic nature and as the days go by, feel free to talk to your friends about your list. You can add to it or take items off, but please make sure that your list is as accurate and honest as you can make it. Then, when the opportunity arises and you are faced with making a decision, pay attention to your feeling comfortable or uncomfortable and act in your long-term best interests.

Chapter 6

If YOU DON'T WORK IT OUT,
YOU'LL ACT IT OUT

My father died when I was twenty-three and while we didn't have a contentious relationship, we did have issues. I blamed him for causing the throat cancer that eventually killed him (he smoked two packs of cigarettes from the time he was a teenager until he was diagnosed with cancer at the age of forty-eight, then continued to smoke two packs a day for the remaining fifteen years of his life). I think he blamed me for the unrest that my generation brought to the 1960s. After he died, I dreamed about him periodically for about seven years, including one dream in which I shot him with a pistol. Obviously, I was still angry with him. Then, one night I dreamed of walking up to him and giving him a hug. Apparently I had resolved things with him because this was the last time I dreamed of him.

I had a distant relationship with my mother who died when I was twenty-two. I don't recall ever dreaming of her, but I know that for years I acted out unresolved issues. Because she never held or cuddled me, my brother, or my two sisters, I developed touch deprivation, which in some cases can be quite serious. I craved human touch and

I was so lucky to have had several girlfriends when I was a teenager who hugged and kissed me. To this day I love going for a massage or having someone give me a back rub. However, even though I dated girls who were warm and enjoyed physical touch, because I did not work out the relationship I had with my mother, I ended up marrying my late wife who hugged and cuddled our three children, but not me and I am sure I played a significant role in that.

Relationships with relatives are some of the most significant we have, but they are by no means the only people that we may have issues with that we need to work out. Close friends, significant others, partners, colleagues, and neighbors often slip into our inner selves and if we are unfortunate enough to have hurt one another or if we have left some issue unresolved, we will probably act it out.

Large issues need work over time and in some instances with the help of a therapist. Smaller issues are often resolved with an honest exchange. When my wife and I have a disagreement, we say, "Can we talk?" Letting each other know how we feel is often sufficient to clear the air. At other times, to avoid creating an issue we'll say, "This is just talk," meaning we're not going to be offended, we won't make a decision just yet, and the purpose of our talking is to see where we stand.

When I started the Northern Virginia Writing Project in 1978, my first secretary told me that her husband was still waking up screaming from nightmares about his experiences in World War II, over thirty years earlier. Today we recognize this as Post Traumatic Stress Syndrome and soldiers coming back from war are routinely advised and treated by therapists. In a similar context, in the early 1970s I met five Vietnam vets who were being treated for PTSD by a local therapist and they said that when they shared their stories with one another, they often cried. At the time, I was shocked at the stories they told about their experiences but looking back on this now, I am so grateful that these vets had an opportunity to work things out. We all know that soldiers coming back from war today are still having a tough time, but at least we're aware of the need to provide help for them.

My late wife's father spent the last five years of his life in a nursing home and in his last year he had worked through and let go of all the things that had bothered him—which from my perspective weren't many, but it's impossible to know what other people carry. His letting go made him a truly beautiful person in his last year and because of that he became an inspiration for me.

Another way to clear out something that is large is the method I used in grieving for my late wife. I jotted down on a sheet of paper all the memorable things of our lives together and then wrote about them one day at a time. This usually works, but when it doesn't, we need the help of a therapist.

Please take a minute to jot down in your journal any of the things you think you think still need to work out. As you know, your journal is private so no one will know unless you decide to talk about it. Then take the next step and set up a strategy and schedule for working these things out and if necessary plan to get in touch with a therapist to help you.

Working Out Small Things On A Daily Basis

In addition to the larger things we have to work out, all of us have experiences throughout the day that leave their mark on us and we need to work out these small things as well. They can range from feeling dissed by an offhanded remark made by a coworker to feeling horny because we passed someone in the hall who was very sexy. Again, if we don't work these things out, we stand a good chance of acting them out. We may arrive home to greet our significant other in a really bad mood or we may arrive home wanting nothing more than to have sex regardless of what our significant other wants.

Of course, the best time to work things out is at the moment they occur. If we say to our coworker, "Hey Ashley, did you really mean you don't think I can handle this contract?" the chances are we will resolve both the misunderstanding and the hurt feelings on the spot. Likewise, if we say to the person in the hall, "Thank you for being so beautiful. You made my day," chances are you'll gain enough distance to stop feeling horny. If we're not comfortable actually saying this to the person, we can say it to ourselves and chances are it will work just as well.

I'm not a therapist, but when people ask me for help in "cleaning out the attic," I try to decide if they need the help of a therapist or if it is small stuff that I can help them with. Minute-by-minute things, as long as they're small, can be paid attention to and resolved on the spot. Recently a friend of mine received a promotion and when I emailed him my congratulations I added, "As my students would say, 'You're tight.'" He emailed me back asking what I meant, and I could tell that for him the word tight meant stingy. I explained that when my students said "tight." they meant unqualified admiration. This quick exchange with my friend resolved any misunderstanding.

How do we know if we have one of these little things to work out? It's relatively simple. If we're still thinking about what happened earlier in the day rather than what's in front of us, we probably need to work it out.

Most of us already have our favorite ways of working out these little things, but just in case let me mention a few that I've seen people use. One way is to work out physically—jogging, sports, yoga—activities that really get us moving. As we exercise, we naturally think about the things we're carrying, and one by one they drop off by themselves. Another way is to dump our thoughts and feelings on a close friend or loved one who is willing to be used for such things. And, of course a third way is to journal, reflect, let go, and meditate.

Whatever method we choose, it needs to be healthy for us. Yes, sometimes getting drunk as a skunk is called for, but we shouldn't make this a frequent choice.

Finally, if the things we have to work out are recurring on a regular basis, we need to hold a business meeting with ourselves and/or those involved. We need to let our coworker who is regularly dissing us know that things have to change and if necessary we'll involve a supervisor to negotiate the discussion.

Once working things out becomes part of our daily routine, we discover ourselves going to bed at night with a smile on our face.

Taking Responsibility for How We're Treated by Others

The scene was quick and simple. It was a Saturday when Ceres and I had lots to do—yard work, chores, and errands. I had done my usual routine of journaling, exercise, and meditation and I was standing in the hall about to go to the hardware store. I was feeling peaceful from sitting and was looking forward to getting some lumber and nails. Ceres, on the other hand, was upset with someone at another store whom she thought had charged her too much for an item she had bought. Within fifteen seconds I blurted out, "Don't pollute my air." She knew exactly what I meant and changed the conversation.

To be honest, I was surprised that I had stood up for myself. That's not how I was raised. More typical of me would have been to listen to her until she had finished venting and then try to help her to return to the store and talk to the clerk in order to feel better about things.

Ceres is far from being a negative person. In fact, she is one of the happiest people I've ever met and her joyous laughter is known throughout our neighborhood. So, this is not a matter of avoiding associating with a person who is not good for me, but rather letting her know that at that particular moment, I didn't want to listen to a stream of negative emotions.

Taking responsibility for how we are treated by others can be very difficult for some of us, especially if we were not raised that way. I think our first step is becoming aware of how we were treated by our family, relatives, and friends. As I said in the previous chapter, most of us enter our teens and early twenties with a pattern of behavior that is comfortable for us. When we learn that some of these behaviors are not in our best interests, it is necessary for us to be uncomfortable for a while in order to grow into a healthier lifestyle and we need to work these things out.

When I have my students work in response groups, I notice that when they and/or their writing is being treated negatively, the way they respond falls into two major categories—ones who take responsibility for how they are being treated and ones who don't. Among those who take responsibility, some of them simply ignore negative comments.

They may say, "Whatever," but then they move on to other students in their group and get what they're looking for, "Okay, that's what Matt thinks—what do you think of my piece, Jennifer?"

Other students get very upset and fight back, often engaging in an argument that wanders off topic.

"You're so wrong. That's not what I was talking about and you know it. You are so off topic. I bet you don't even know how to order a chicken sandwich. No wonder you didn't bring copies of your writing for us to read." Despite the negative reaction, they are standing up for themselves.

Yet another group of students will listen to a negative response and then hold a discussion on what their classmate is talking about.

"So, you're saying you don't like reading pieces about athletes who have started their own businesses. Is that right?"

"Yes."

"And that's because you think athletes should just be athletes. Is that right?"

"Yes. All I care about is what they do on the field. The rest just doesn't matter."

"Well, I then have two choices. I can still write about athletes, but not ones who have started their own businesses or I can stick with the group of athletes I have here and get feedback from readers who like this topic."

"Yeah, I suppose you can do that."

"Actually, I have a better idea now of who I'm writing to. So, thanks for helping me."

Then there are students who do not take responsibility for how they are being treated. For example, I had one student who just put up with the negative comments of one of her classmates until she became so upset that she ran out of the classroom crying. Obviously, I transferred her to another group and spoke to the student who had offended her, but I also mentored my student for the next several weeks on ways to respond to negative comments.

I am aware that taking responsibility for how we're treated and working things out are very complex issues and that there are times when we as individuals, just as we as nations, can only go just so far. A spouse can stand up for his or her rights, but may still get nasty letters from his or her ex. A customer can ask for help in finding an item in a store, but may still get dissed by an employee and a homeowner may ask that people clean up after their dogs have messed up their sidewalk, but the dog owners don't always comply. How we treat ourselves at this point depends not on others, but on ourselves.

Again, the trick is to become comfortable with taking responsibility for how we're treated by others. This may take practice, but we can do it.

Please take a minute to jot down your usual way of taking responsibility for how you're treated and feel free to share these things with a close and caring friend. After your discussion, if you would like to keep, change, or add strategies, please do and keep track of your experiences so that you get good at taking care of yourself.

Chapter 7

OPEN YOUR EYES. WHAT YOU ARE LOOKING FOR IS RIGHT IN FRONT OF YOU

I am lucky; I am not lucky. I am fulfilled; I am deprived. I am blessed; I am cursed. At any given moment, I am one or the other of each dichotomy.

So what determines which one?

Whether or not my eyes are open.

Being open-eyed is a mental state, but that mental state also has an influence physically on how I am seeing what is right in front of me.

Am I different from anyone else? No. All humans experience the exact same thing.

When our mental and physical eyes are closed, we cannot see what is right in front of us.

My wife Ceres and I had finished dinner a few minutes earlier and it was at the end of a very long but average day. During the commute to and from work, I had listened to the news and various talk shows—and to be honest, I turned off the radio several times because I was fed up with one report after another about individuals fighting, groups fighting, nations fighting—it seemed like everyone was fighting. I just wanted everyone to get along. I carried that desire with me as we did what we usually do after dinner—relax in the living room and continue our conversation. We have no television in that room so it is just the two of us and of course Pinot and Harlow, our two cats, who follow us into the room to play with one another and us.

As I sat down, I knew I was carrying with me my desire of wanting everyone to get along and I also knew it was interfering with our evening. So, instead I opened my eyes to see what was in front of me. What I saw was two young cats playing with a toy, taking turns chasing it, keeping an eye on each other, watching out for each other. I also saw an incredibly beautiful woman listening and talking with me, the both of us sharing stories from our day. On the walls were drawings and various pieces of art, beautifully arranged. In effect, what I was looking for—for everyone to get along—was right there.

What do I mean when I say, "Open your eyes"? Being present, seeing with your senses, seeing with your whole being. As humans, we actually need very little to be happy. As I mentioned previously, we need love, food, shelter, and a certain amount of health. These are the basic things we're really looking for. When I want "everyone to get along", I am asking for world peace. World peace has to start somewhere and for each one of us it starts with one step. That night in my living room, it started for me when I became at peace with myself.

Levels Of Consciousness

I am standing at the kitchen sink, rinsing a dish, the hot water running over my hands. It is close to 7:30 on a Monday morning. I have already written briefly in my journal and have sat on the sofa in the den to meditate for twenty minutes. It was a typical meditation with lots of thoughts in the first five minutes and then a decreasing number of thoughts until they became well spaced out. The peace between each one was refreshing and because of this my eyes were open.

As I stand at the sink, I hear Ceres come into the kitchen. My back is to her and I hear her say, "Good morning, Sunshine."

I turn around and reply, "Hello, Love."

Suddenly, at the core of my being I feel a gush of love, the same feeling that accompanied my falling in love with her when we first met. I am surprised. Yes, I love my wife, but it had been years since I've had this feeling that I associate with the beginning of our relationship.

As you would expect, research has already been done on states of being or as some call it, levels of consciousness. David R. Hawkins in his book *Power vs. Force* lists the following seventeen levels:

- Enlightenment
- Peace
- Joy
- Love
- Reason
- Acceptance
- Willingness
- Neutrality
- Courage
- Pride
- Anger
- Desire
- Fear
- Grief
- Apathy
- Guilt
- Shame

While some of us may quibble with one being higher than another, I don't think any of us would argue that enlightenment, peace, joy, and love are higher than desire, fear, guilt, and shame. And for me, the process of lifting oneself up the ladder is a process of letting go and opening my eyes. These two activities allow me to experience states of being listed at the top of David Hawkins' list.

Several months ago, one of my neighbors became upset with me for parking my car on the street in front of her house. She said she had a crew coming that would be doing something in her yard and they would probably need the street in front of her house to part their truck. At first I was hurt that she was upset with me, but as I let it go, I said to her, "I would be glad to move my car." And I did. In effect, because I was in the habit of letting go, I was able to let go of the feelings that swelled up inside of me when she was upset with me. While I'm not sure I would label the feeling I had for her at the moment as love, I would say that I did feel compassion and I definitely had no trouble being kind to her.

Before reading the next section, please let go and open your eyes as you interact with people, then see what impact this has on your levels of consciousness. As always, remember to take a moment to jot down your thoughts in your journal.

Intuition

I was standing in the grocery store, starring at a red pepper. Something was telling me I needed to buy the pepper, but my rational mind said, "Are you nuts? You don't need a red pepper." So, I listened to my rational mind, turned away from the red pepper, bought my other groceries, and went home.

After putting the fresh vegetables in the refrigerator and the canned goods in the pantry, I took out one of my cookbooks and soon found a recipe that I really wanted to make for dinner.

"Oh, no," I said. "One of the ingredients is a red pepper."

As the saying goes, I felt like kicking myself. Instead, I decided to do something that I hoped might save me from making the same mistake in the future. Because I had been in the store only about twenty minutes earlier, I was able to recall the feeling I had when I was staring at the red pepper and I did my best to place that feeling into long-term memory. If this were to happen again, I wanted to know enough to buy the damn pepper.

By now, I can usually, but not always, tell when my intuition is turned on and trying to tell me something. The problem I have is that there are still times when I don't listen to it. Just today I headed out to buy a flashlight bulb and I had two choices of where to buy it—the large hardware store or the small one. My rational mind said, "Large one—more choice and therefore a better chance it will have the right one." My intuitive mind said, "Small one." That's all. "Small one." Of course, being intuition, it did not follow up with a reason why I should go to the small hardware store. Yup, you know. When I got to the large hardware store there were plenty of flashlights including one like the one I had at home. I took the burned-out bulb that I had brought along with me out of my pocket and looked at the bulbs they had available. They had two that were one size smaller and one that was one size larger, but none that were the size I needed. When I asked for help, the employee checked the shelf, called his manager, then turned to me and said, "I'm sorry. We're out of them." So, I drove over to the small hardware store and sure enough, the right-sized bulb was there.

More recently, I went to the grocery store and walked right up to a bottle of Riesling. I picked it up, held it in my hand, and rather than trust my intuition, I listened to my rational mind that was saying, "You don't drink Riesling and you have plenty of white wine at home." So I placed the bottle back on the shelf, picked up a few other things, and went home. As I began to prepare dinner, I looked in the refrigerator and saw some summer squash soup that I had made earlier in the week. "It would be nice to have this with dinner, but we've had it for the past two nights so I need to change it somehow." Almost immediately it hit me—I could serve it cold rather than hot and all I would need is some Riesling to it to give it a much different taste. Yup, back to the store.

You would think that listening to my intuition would be easy for me because I meditate, but as the above examples show, it isn't. My day is filled with rational activities. It's a huge part of both my professional life and my home life. People expect me to back things up with reasons why I say something and I expect the same from others. For instance, I expect my doctor to examine my knee, ask me to walk in front of her, take an x-ray—and only then to say, "Worn cartilage." Even if she had thought "worn cartilage" when I walked into the room, I still would have wanted her to back up her intuition and give me reasons for her diagnosis.

Fortunately, there are times when I do listen to my intuition and when I do it's as if I open both my physical eyes and my spiritual eyes. One day I had a gift that I wanted to drop off for Linda and something told me to do it in the middle of the day. My rational mind said, "No, that's okay. You can drop it off tonight and if she's not home you can just leave it on her porch." The persistent feeling of "Do it now," made no sense. I thought, *She won't be at home now because she works all day and if I leave it on her porch, chances were good that it will get rained on or blown away by the wind.* So, I ignored reason, drove to her house, walked up to her front door and as I rang the doorbell I looked for a place on her porch where I could leave it where it would be safe. *Nowhere*, I concluded. Then all of a sudden, I heard the door being unlocked from the inside. It was her cleaning lady. I didn't know Linda had a cleaning lady. I gave her the gift and asked her to place it on Linda's kitchen table.

When it comes to intuition, I'm pretty much self-taught. As far as I can remember, my earliest experience with it was when I was around ten or eleven. I was a boy scout and our troop staged a little game where the scoutmaster had us stand in a field with the assistant scoutmasters while he went into the woods to hide a silver dollar. The scout who found the coin would win a turkey for his family for Thanksgiving. About ten minutes later, the scoutmaster came out of the woods and yelled, "Go get it." I walked into the woods and within a minute found the coin. The scoutmaster couldn't believe it. He thought I had seen him hide the coin. He huddled together with the assistant scoutmasters, then said, "Okay, we're going to do this over." So once again, we stood in the field and this time he made sure that we were all facing the opposite direction. He went into the woods, hid the coin, came back out of the woods and said, "Go!"

Again I walked into the woods, bent down, and picked it up.

Later that afternoon, I was home when the scoutmaster called my father to let him know I had won a Thanksgiving turkey for my family. I don't know if he told my father what had happened, but either way what I had done was not, for me, that much out of the ordinary.

Throughout my life when I need to find something, I do. My wife wanted to know where to open her family counseling practice so I drove to the town she was considering, turned on my intuition, and drove to the building where I knew she would work. Sure enough, that was the very building where she had her practice for years.

My guess is that we all have intuition, but to varying degrees. Those of us with incredibly strong intuition are called psychics. I've gone to psychics from time to time and they know things that there is no rational way to explain. One psychic told me that my father-in-law would pass away in a few years, which was not surprising to me because he had a terminal illness and was living in a nursing home. She then said that there was someone on the other side waiting for him, someone with a limp. I knew my father-in-law well enough to know some of his friends and as far as I could recall, none of them had a limp.

When I got home I told my late wife what the psychic had told me and she said, "Oh that's my dad's best friend. He passed away a number of years ago and he was a cripple."

There are lots of benefits to listening to your intuition and the one I like the best is that it is a very valuable source of information. We all use the internet to get answers to our questions—from small to large—and we would never think of not using it when we need it, but intuition is also helpful to have. From the several books I've read on intuition, including Sonia Choquette's *Trust Your Vibes*, it's important that we use our sixth sense wisely.

On page 47 she writes, "If your intuitive channel is open but your tuner isn't dialed to your Higher Self, you may accidentally pick up on that negative energy without even knowing it."

She advises us to keep our distance from people with bad moods and walk away from negative conversations.

Sonia also recommends that we get some friends to support us because sixth sensory people don't do well alone. As I read this in her book, I so agreed with her that I said a quick prayer for help in finding some people who would be willing to meditate with me and to share experiences they had using intuition. That same evening at a dinner with some friends and without my having anything to do with it, the conversation drifted to the subject of meditation.

Then one of them said, "I can't meditate alone. I need other people to help me."

The person sitting beside her said, "Let's get together once a week so we can meditate together."

I was amazed and immediately remembered the brief prayer I had said only eight hours earlier.

"I would love join you," I added and with that, the three of us set a date.

Regardless of your degree of intuition, consider paying attention to your sixth sense. Start off doing what I did the afternoon I gazed at the red pepper—identify what it feels like when your intuition is working. I also recommend that you read a few books on this subject so that you can strengthen your intuition. And finally, get together with some like-minded friends with whom you can share your journey.

Chapter 8

DO WHAT GIVES YOU ENERGY

Most of us love to do what gives us energy. We may have days when we feel depleted rather than energized, but overall we try to do those things that give us energy. For some of us, doing these things means following in the footsteps of ancestors. Brain research is telling us that our activities become part of our DNA, so it is not surprising to have an extended family consisting mostly of teachers, engineers, accountants, electricians, or artists. Yes, it's possible that a dislocation or emigration may interrupt such a line making it temporarily impossible to have a first or second job choice, but in time that returns. Sometimes we even find a way of turning our job into our desired activity—as when an electrician who gets his energy from teaching others, finds a way to teach budding electricians.

I think we are born headed in a particular direction and we are happiest when we discover it and follow it. If we're not inclined to trust our own instincts, we may have to rely on the help of others. As I said earlier, it wasn't until my sophomore year of college that I knew I would become a teacher and it took a classmate of mine telling me, "Don, you're going to be a teacher," for me to get it. Some of us need the help of career counselors, tests such as the Myers Briggs test, and both friends and family members. We know we're in the right job when we feel good about it, when we're energized by a day's work, and when we look forward to growing in the profession we've selected.

Another thing that can give us energy is the way we go about our lives on a day-to-day basis. A friend of mine is a master at emotional intelligence and at holding a conversation in which both he and others feel great about being listened to. He has a way of acknowledging and affirming our statements, adding to them, and responding in a way that moves the conversation forward at just the right pace. I have another friend who moves through his day very focused, ignoring distractions and returning to the chores he has scheduled himself. I have a third friend who loves music and it is always on in the background. You can tell that it is his first choice of attention because he is always humming along with it. Ceres loves things and she sees the world as the perfect place to decorate. When we go on vacation, she can't wait to shop. Even when she doesn't buy anything, she loves going from store to store to look at one item after another. For all these people, these daily activities give them energy.

Just as all of us have experiences with jobs or activities that give us energy, we all have experiences that drain us of energy. Introverts find it exhausting to be around people for extended periods of time, just as extroverts find it tiring to be alone. For them, solitary confinement is hell. Because there are no absolutes in what gives us energy or takes it away, it is up to each of us to take responsibility for moving our lives in a direction that is healthy for us. For some of us, this is not easy. I know a colleague who listened to a presentation for eight hours, when what she really wanted to do was listen for thirty minutes, give feedback, and then move on with her day. For some people it would have been easy to say, "I'm sorry. I really wish I could spend my whole day listening to your presentation, but I have things I just have to get done. I'll tell you what I see so far and I hope that will be enough to be of some help."

Where do we pick up the ability to stand up for what gives us energy? Some of us are born into families that make such statements on a daily basis. I recently saw a young mother at the beach tell her two-year old daughter, "Play with your toys until your little heart is content." The child did just that—playing in the sand in the most peaceful manner.

A little while later, the daughter called out to her father who was standing at the edge of the water, "Don't fall in the ocean, Dad."

My wife turned to me and said, "They could charge admission for this."

Before we left the beach, we saw the daughter ironing her mom's back with her little toy iron.

Doing what gives us energy and avoiding what depletes us takes courage—courage to stand up for what is truly important to us. Courage wouldn't be courage if it were easy, yet being courageous eventually gives us a life filled with peace, joy, and happiness.

Please take a minute to make a list of the things that give you energy, as well as a list of things that rob you of energy. Keep these lists in mind as you go through your day and whenever possible, gravitate toward those things that give you energy.

Learning New Things Gives Us Energy

One of the things I enjoy most about my marriage to Ceres is our sharing the things we've learned from reading newspapers, professional articles, and current research. Consequently, our discussions at dinner and afterwards as we sit in the living room are very engaging and there is always something new for each of us in our conversations.

In addition, from time to time we both wake up in the middle of the night and spend some time chatting. Because we are relaxed from having slept three or four hours, our conversations also are relaxed as we share our thoughts and opinions about things going on around us and in the news. I tell her how delighted I am to have read an article in the newspaper in which a state comptroller is advocating for high schools to offer a course on financial responsibility. She tells me about an interview on NPR with Johnny Cash's daughter in which she talked about how important it was that her dad had left her a list of his favorite country songs.

Why does this work for us? How is it that we are constantly learning something new from each other? One reason is that we are constantly learning something new each day from our jobs, from our friends, from things going on in the world, and from our beloved cats. In addition, an even deeper reason is that we are both going through life with our eyes open.

If we approach life and each other with "the same old" mentality, we will be miserable. On weekends, when we're not going out with friends, I like to have dinner at 6:30 PM. That gives me enough time to prepare a good meal and then leaves us several hours to watch a movie, take a walk, or do a host of other things that we both enjoy. Ceres could very well say, "Oh, no. Not 6:30 again!" Likewise, on an almost daily basis she asks me if a certain blouse goes with a particular skirt. As far as I know, she has never asked me for my opinion on the same blouse and skirt combination but I could very well say to her, "Oh no, not again. You're always asking me for my opinion on what goes with what!"

For us, seeing each moment as one we have never lived before enables us to both appreciate it and also to learn from it and both of these things give us energy. Yes, they may be little things, but they're more than enough to make our lives exciting.

On a larger scale, it is equally important for everyone to be involved in learning something new on an ongoing, regular basis. This may involve taking a class such as the one Ceres once took on gardening or my hanging out with an electrician as he fixed a faulty outlet so that I could learn how one circuit influenced another. In our jobs, there are always new approaches that we are studying and these involve our going to conferences and reading the latest research. All these things give us energy.

One of the differences between the learning that takes place when you are in school working toward a degree and learning after you've graduated is that if you don't have to take a class, you are much more likely to choose a class or area of learning that will solve a problem you're encountering. Ceres grew up in a city and had little contact with gardens, so for her a gardening class was perfect. For me, having a childhood in which I did absolutely no electrical work made it perfect for me to hang out with an electrician.

Learning new things is much more important that we might at first expect. For one, we end up with a much larger understanding of the world around us and that in itself makes us much more interesting to be around, more understanding and compassionate of others, and lessens our tendency to see the world as "us versus them". Furthermore, learning new things makes us smarter so that when we encounter a new situation, we have a wide variety of approaches to choose from.

The bottom line is that if we're bored, we need to get ourselves into a situation where we'll learn something new. In addition, we also need to check our curiosity. If it has diminished of late, we need to explore something totally new. Yes, initially we'll feel a little uncomfortable, but after a while we'll grow. Ceres just asked me to add the experience we had in India when I taught the Dalai Lama's Buddhist monks how to write. They were amazing students and due to their daily practice of meditation, they laughed and played like children as they went about learning new things.

Take a moment to brainstorm a list of things you want to learn and how you want to go about learning them. If possible, place a few of these items in your day planner.

Doing What Gives You Energy Also Makes You Happy

As you know from reading the previous chapters, I've meditated since the early 70s, I've exercised since I was a kid in the 1940s, and I've kept a journal since 1979. Why? Exercise keeps me healthy, enables me to play with members of my family, and makes it possible for me to fix things around the house. Keeping a journal gives me a place to dump my thoughts—especially negative thoughts from the previous day. And meditation makes it possible for me to focus, be more efficient, and avoid doing stupid things for which I would later have to apologize. Have I done these things to be happy? I guess so, but I never thought about it until recently.

Due to my compartmentalized thinking, I've always associated happiness with certain activities such as teaching, being with people I love, cooking, and eating, but I haven't connected it with the focused mind that comes about as a result of journaling, exercising, and meditating. When I read John Tierney's article in *The Washington Post* about a study conducted by Matthew A. Killingsworth and Daniel T. Gilbert, "A Wandering Mind Is an Unhappy Mind", I began to make the connection.

You would think I would have made the connection based on an experience I had when I drove five hours from North Carolina to Northern Virginia. We left at 7:00 PM and the weather was on and off very rainy—even at times so stormy that it was difficult to see out the front window. Ceres was tired and spent most of the trip napping.

I purposely did not turn on the radio because I didn't want to be distracted or to wake her up. Instead, for five hours straight I paid attention to one thing—driving. When we arrived home around midnight, I was very calm and peaceful. If you had asked it if I were also happy, I would have paused then said, "Yes," but I would have been thinking, *Why are you asking me that? I was just driving my car.*

The way Killingsworth and Gilbert conducted their study is interesting. They used an iPhone app called TrackYourHappiness and called more than 2,200 people around the world at random intervals to ask them how they were feeling. From 250,000 responses, they learned that people were happiest in the following activities listed here in descending order: sex, exercising, conversation, listening to music, taking a walk, eating, praying and meditating, cooking, shopping, taking care of their children, reading—and at the bottom of the long list, personal grooming, commuting, and working. Because I love my job, I would place working much higher on my list, but I fully agree that commuting for me is on the bottom.

Another of Killingsworth and Gilbert's findings is that the minds of the people they contacted were wandering forty-seven percent of the time. Wow! If I were part of the study, I am sure that that would be way above my percentage. I would say that my mind is wandering about ten percent of the time—at most. And I attribute my ability to stay focused to my doing things that give me energy.

I'm guessing that most, if not all of us agree that doing things that give us energy also makes us happy, but please take a moment to make your own list of activities in descending order that make you happy. This may end up the same list of things that are on your list of things that give you energy and if so, that's fine. If there are differences between the two lists, take a moment to explore the reasons your lists are different.

Chapter 9

COME TO YOUR RELATIONSHIP RUNNING ON FULL, NOT EMPTY

I had spent Wednesday by myself, working from home. From 7:00-10:00 AM I did office work, emails, and reports. Then when Ceres left for work, I went to the bookstore where I read student papers until 1:00 P.M. I came home and did a mixture of preparing for class, writing letters of recommendation, doing office work, writing reports, and answering emails until around 7:30 when I prepared dinner. When Ceres came home at 8:30, I was really glad to see her. We had a wonderful dinner and then we sat in the living room and talked about our day.

The next morning, I was still feeling a little lonely from the previous day that I had spent mostly by myself. Before getting ready to go to work, I followed my usual routine by writing in my journal, exercising, and meditating for twenty minutes. When I went into the kitchen to make salad for lunch, Ceres asked me a question and I said something to which she replied, "Jawohl," which is German for "Yes", especially if you are a soldier who is responding to an order given by your superior. Yes, my ancestors were German and yes, I have a strict side to me, but because I was still feeling depleted, I resented her comment. I didn't say anything because I was in a hurry, but before I got to work I took out my cell phone to call her to let her know that I felt uncomfortable with her comment. Between ring one and ring four, I realized that the reason I was feeling uncomfortable was because I had not taken sufficient care of myself after suffering from a sense isolation the day before. So I hung up and figured it was my job to fill up my own tank. Surprisingly, she called back and asked if I had called.

"Yes," I said.

"We're out of dishwasher detergent so if you're going to the grocery store sometime today, could you pick some up?"

"I'd be glad to," I said and then before hanging up I said, "Love you."

"Love you too," she replied.

As I drove to work, I was already feeling better. I was still running on low, but at least I wasn't running on empty. When I walked into the office, I had a question for Stephanie.

"Why is it that I don't really care for most of the music I hear on the radio, but then there will be a string of about ten songs that I really like. It's as if the person who selected those songs had asked me beforehand."

"I don't know," she said, "but I know how you can find songs you like."

With that, she walked me through the website called Pandora and showed me how to set up an account and how to select songs. It took no more than a few minutes and I was delighted.

A while later, I walked over to the Dean's office to ask the finance people a question about salaries and they were so helpful. When I returned, I asked Mark a question about speakers for a one-day conference that the College of Health and Human Sciences was having and he quickly came up with the name of a writer in that field. When I emailed Margaret, the professor who had asked for help with finding someone, she was so happy to get my suggestion.

When I went to class at 3:00 P.M., I saw one of my students who was struggling with completing her assignments on time because she had had one cold after another. I was so glad to see her and after a brief conversation I knew she was eager to get her work done. Finally, a committee meeting that met from 4:30-6:00 went very well because my colleagues had done an excellent job writing their reports.

I arrived home around 7:30 that evening and because of all these wonderful events during the day, I was running on full. Ceres and I had a wonderful conversation, a delicious dinner, and I was glad to help her plan an event that was coming up.

Please take a minute to recall a similar experience where events during the day allowed you to come to your significant other running on full, not empty.

Selecting Your Own Gas Station

A few weeks ago, I realized that the chair I had in front of my desk at home was great for when I was working on my computer, but when I had to read manuscripts, articles, or books over a long period of time, it was uncomfortable. At work I had a chair that was tall enough that I could tilt it back, rest my legs on the desk, and read for hours. I wanted the same thing at home, so one afternoon after a relatively hard day at work, I stopped by Costco to check out their office chairs.

Costco had three models—two that were made of leather and one made of cloth. The cloth one was not very comfortable, was a bit small, and was a murky gray—the wrong color for my office at home that had soft gold walls, a maroon sofa, and a deep walnut-colored desk. The two leather chairs were made by Lane, with the smaller one going for about $150 and the larger one for about $250. I slid them down onto the floor from the platform they were resting on and tried them out. The smaller of the two was a bit firmer, but oh so comfortable, especially on my back. The larger one was easier on my legs and had a cuddly headrest. I moved from chair to chair, tilting back and forth in each one, spinning around in circles, resting my legs on my shopping cart, staring up at the ceiling as if deep in thought, and holding my hands in my lap as if I were reading a book. I spent about fifteen minutes there, smiling with deep contentment as shoppers rolled by. In the end, I left without buying either one because I wanted to try moving another chair I had at home into my office and using that one instead.

After a long, hard day at work, those fifteen minutes in Costco restored my spirit. It felt whole again, almost pampered. I had treated myself to listening to my feelings and doing something totally for me. The residual effect was that when I arrived home, I was one happy camper. I made dinner and had a warm and engaging conversation with my wife.

About a week later, I had a similar hard day at the office and this time, instead of stopping off to check out office chairs, I tried to beat the traffic. Not surprisingly, I got caught in rush hour, at times not moving at all, at other times creeping along at five miles an hour. The news on the radio was "the same old" as my students would describe it and the music was equally irritating. Needless to say, I arrived home depleted. I slopped food together to resemble dinner, held a jerky conversation with my wife, and left the kitchen wishing I were in Costco.

No, it is not always possible to come to a relationship running on full, but obviously it is the best way if at all possible. As we all know, it is not our partner's responsibility to fill our gas tank—it is our responsibility. Sometimes Ceres is warm and cuddly and that fills me up, but it is not part of our contract. I am the one, and the only one, who is ultimately responsible for my life and that includes my portion of our relationship. When I accept that responsibility and act on it, our relationship may or may not work, but at least I've done my part.

We all can relate to this gas tank analogy—and everyone reading this has had a day when they felt like they should pull over because they're about to run out of gas. Just as all of us have had days when we are so happy that we feel as if we could conquer the world.

The first step in coming to a relationship running on full is being honest with ourselves. It does us no good to pretend that we have any more in our tanks than we actually do. If we happen to be running on low, it's important that we just acknowledge that. It's equally important to not exaggerate our neediness. This is not the time to exercise narcissism.

The second step is to know where our gas station is and to get ourselves there. For me, one way is stopping by a store as in my Costco experience. I don't have to buy anything—I just have to pamper myself. Of course, there will be times when we will need to ask our significant other for permission to do so because he or she may also need to go to a gas station. If the same experience replenishes both of you, that's even better. As long as we're being honest, in most cases our significant other will say, "Yes".

The third step is to fill up the tank. No bullshit, no dallying, no avoidance. Just fill up the tank. Then we need to return to our significant other and do our part in making the relationship the best it can be. Is this at times hard as hell? Yes. Is it worth the effort? You bet.

Earlier you wrote about an experience where a series of events during the day allowed you to come to your significant other running on full. This time, make a list of things you can do pretty much whenever needed to fill up your tank.

Full, But Not Overflowing

It was a Sunday. Ceres and I had spent the weekend on the beach in Rehoboth jogging on the sand, reading books, and gazing at the ocean. On the drive back to Virginia, we stopped in the small town of Lewes to do a quick tour. We had just arrived when I got a call from Ann, my tenant and friend who lived in the little cottage behind our house. She was calling to tell me that the spout in the tub in her bathroom was working, but when she pulled the little lever to make the water come out the showerhead, it didn't work. In effect, she had no shower.

I was always happy to hear from her, even when she was calling to tell me something needed fixing. On her side, she knew I liked it when she called me about a problem while it was still small rather than waiting until the problem had grown beyond my ability to fix it by myself.

"I'll be back tonight and I'll take a look at it in the morning," I told her.

On Monday morning, right after Ann left for work, I did just that. Sure enough, when I pulled on the little lever at the front end of the spout, the water continued to spurt out of the spout with none of it shooting up into the showerhead. I had never worked on a bathtub spout, so I went to my plumber.

After I described the situation, I said, "Is this something I can fix?"

"Oh yeah. It's easy. Some spouts just unscrew and others you have to loosen the screw on it from underneath and then you just pull it off. Just crawl underneath to see if it has a screw."

"I can do that," I said. "Do I bring it here to get a replacement?"

"No—take it to the plumbing supply store. They'll have it."

I was already feeling better. It sounded like this was something I could do myself. When I got back to the cottage, I crawled into the tub, looked up under the spout, and sure enough, it had a screw. I went back to my toolbox, got the right screwdriver, crawled back into the tub, loosened the screw, crawled out of the tub, and slid the spout off the pipe. I was starting to feel happy. This was much easier than I had expected.

I then took the spout to the plumbing supply store where the clerk took one look at it and said, "Diverter spout, slip fit, 5/8 inch."

He walked back to one of the shelves and returned with a small white box.

Before I paid for it I asked him, "Can I take a look at it?"

"Of course."

I opened the box and sure enough it was identical to the one I had removed from Ann's tub.

Replacing it was simple. I just slid it onto the pipe and tightened the screw. When I turned on the water and pulled the diverter (I now knew what to call it), the water gushed out of the shower.

The whole job had taken me about an hour from start to finish.

For those of you who are not familiar with home repairs, it usually takes hours for the simplest jobs and most home repair guys make about three trips to the hardware store. This was one of the easiest I had ever done and I felt so happy that everything had worked so smoothly. Yes, I had enough experience to know to ask for advice from an expert plumber, but there were no glitches as there often are in routine home repair jobs.

The rest of my day went pretty much as planned—office work, emails, phone calls, and committee reports and around 5:00 P.M. I found a few minutes to meditate. I was not surprised that my first thoughts were of repairing the spout. Yes, I still felt happy about it, so they were very satisfying thoughts. What did surprise me, however, is that one spout-repair thought after the other kept coming as if I had not just let the previous one go. Over and over and over. You would have thought I had been traumatized with happiness. It wasn't until a few hours later near the end of a yoga class I was taking that the spout-repair thoughts subsided.

That evening, when Ceres and I shared our day with each other, I was still very happy but thank goodness I had been able to let go of much of my excitement otherwise I would have gone on and on and on about the spout repair.

The bottom line is that coming to a relationship running on full also means not having a tank that is overflowing. If you have an incredibly wonderful day, see if you can let go of at least some of it so that you can also focus on your relationship.

Take a minute to recall times when you've come to your relationship with an overflowing tank, then jot down some of the things that happened as a result of this. If you can, come up with ways you can remove some of the overflow before your next experience.

Being Aware of the Judge

All of us have ways of thinking that drain our gas tanks and it's important to know what they are so we can protect ourselves. Allow me to tell you about one that I have.

One day Ceres came to me and said, "Ashley's not home. I think I'll let her dog out."

"I think she's home," I said.

"Her car's not in her driveway," Ceres replied.

"Did you look to see if she parked on the street?"

"No."

A short while later Ceres said, "Ashley's home. I knocked on her door and was just about to open it when she answered the door."

"I thought you said you checked to see if her car was on the street."

"I did, but not far enough."

As it turns out, Ashley's car was about thirty feet beyond where Ceres had looked.

I don't know about you, but I experience about five instances like this every day with people I encounter or events I hear about in the news. If Ceres had just glanced up the street she would have spotted

Ashley's car and I would have said to myself, *Well, that was smart.* Because she didn't, I said to myself, *Hmmm. That wasn't smart.*

What I actually said to Ceres was, "Oh, Ashley might have wanted the driveway free for her daughter to park in. Becca is coming home this weekend."

A few weeks after this, Ceres decided to give our house a thorough cleaning—something it had not had in a while. By thorough I mean she moved furniture, rugs, and appliances—just about everything so that she could vacuum, mop, and polish. It was an amazing feat and it took her two full days. The house smelled so sweet and clean, the furniture glowed as it reflected the light, and even the cats were walking around cautiously because they knew things had changed. It was amazing.

I told her, "This is incredible! The house so needed it."

My labeling such actions are acts of my judge and this labeling, whether negative or positive, is similar to the labeling I do when I identify a thought during meditation so that I can let it go. And while my judgments are fine as long as I keep negative thoughts to myself, I need to move beyond such judgments so that I can keep my judge under control.

Without exception, all humans do things that someone can label smart, just as all humans do things that someone can label stupid. While one person is gifted with one kind of intelligence, say spatial intelligence, another may be gifted with emotional intelligence. Doctors are known to be intellectually smart, but even they joke about how the MD at the end of their names stands for "Money Dumb." I'm not a medical doctor, but I too tend to be "Money Dumb." I figure that if I have enough money for such things as food, shelter, transportation, and clothing, I don't have to invest in stocks or do other such things. Knowing that this is not in my best interests, I therefore ask others who are "Money Smart" to help me with my finances.

When it comes to our own well being, it is important that we feel and show compassion and understanding to others. Not only are we all in this world together, our constant and negative judging of others can grow to the point where it will harm even us. We may even end up isolating ourselves if we become too judgmental.

As I mentioned earlier, one way to deal with this is to play a game in which you predict how many instances of intelligence or stupidity you will encounter in a given day. Such a game is not only fun, it gives you distance. It's important, however, that you also let go of your judgments—actually saying to myself, "Okay, that's your judge speaking. Say 'Goodbye, judge. Nice knowing you.'" When this becomes habitual, you can begin the process of seeing without judging and seeing without judging leads me to a direct perception of reality.

Another thing that helps weaken your judge is to write in your journal about a recurring judgment that you're having. When you write about being judgmental of other drivers during your commute, you discover that you were bored and were looking for someone who was driving smartly so that you could be excited and happier. I once saw a driver in a yellow Mercedes doing such a great job of passing people, of signaling at just the right times and of alternating her speed from slow to fast, fast to slow that I followed her for several miles. Because I now know that my boredom during my commute activates my judge, I plan ahead and listen to a challenging CD or an engaging discussion on the radio.

By the way, comparing and contrasting, even stereotyping, are absolutely essential for a safe and healthy existence. What I'm talking here about is using the judge in us when it is not in our best interests.

So, give it a try. Listen to yourself when your judge is activated, see what you can do to move beyond him and see how this allows you to keep running on full when you come to your relationship.

Chapter 10

STRENGTH, STEADINESS, AND FLEXIBILITY

It is a summer afternoon. I am twelve and I have spent the morning mowing the lawn and doing various other chores. It is now around four in the afternoon and I have been shooting arrows since 1:00 PM in my backyard at a target about seventy-five feet away. My mind is at peace as I sink arrow after arrow into the yellow bull's eye.

I received my first bow as a birthday present from my parents when I was about eight or nine. Because they had grown up in Brooklyn and worked in New York City until they were in their early thirties, they probably had little or no experience with archery, yet without knowing it, they gave me the gift that began my spiritual life.

By the time I was twelve, I was spending my Saturday afternoons and several days a week during the summer shooting for about three hours each time I practiced. My father had built me a stand for the large circular straw target that I kept in the garage and I lugged both to the far end of the lawn before shooting.

I do not remember my early experiences with archery, but by the time I was twelve I noticed that during the first hour I was thinking about such things as who I met at the dance the previous night, what happened in history class on Wednesday, and the help I received from the librarian after school—and I missed the target as often as I hit it. During the second hour, my mind became more focused and I hit the target more often. Then in the third hour, my mind was crystal clear and I was sinking arrow after arrow into the bull's eye. There were even a few times when I felt as if I were sitting on the arrow as it glided the seventy-five feet to the target. I also remember one afternoon when I decided I needed a much smaller target than the yellow bull's eye so I picked the notch of the arrow that was already in the target and guess what—I hit it, splitting the arrow halfway down. Because I knew I was the one who would have to replace it, I didn't do that again.

I never talked to anyone about the calm and focused mind I had experienced during the third hour of shooting. Not that I wanted to keep it a secret—it's just that it never occurred to me to share it. I also never thought it was special. I just thought that it was the way archery was for everyone.

In addition to different states of consciousness, I also learned from this experience that if I were to hit the target I had to have strength in both my arms. Because I was right-handed, I held the bow in my left hand and that hand had to be steady. If it shook or moved, there was no chance I would hit the bull's eye. My right hand had to be just as strong, but because it was the hand that was pulling back the string, it had to be flexible. Of course, hours and hours of practice made it possible for me to shoot with incredible steadiness in my left arm and flexibility in my right.

I don't know when I began to transfer this concept of strength, steadiness, and flexibility to other parts of my life and I can't say that archery was the only source of my awareness of these three things, but I do know that by the time I graduated from high school, they were part of my daily approach to life. In order for me to do well in my classes, I had to do my homework. How I did my homework was open to a variety of things (reading the textbook, taking notes, talking to my classmates, reading additional materials, writing a response to the author, drawing a scene, etc.). I also applied this approach to my relationships with others—in effect, to maintain a friendship I had to keep in touch. How I kept in touch depended on the relationship and ranged from phone calls to dates to hanging out.

When I became a parent, I also applied this concept to how I raised my children. For instance, when John, Brendan, and Marisa were teenagers, I had two rules: they were not to get pregnant, nor were they to get anyone else pregnant and they had to let me know where they were. If they went to a party and then went on to another party, they had to call me to let me know where they were going. They had enormous freedom within these restrictions, but the restrictions held firm.

Describing strength, steadiness, and flexibility is easy. Doing it is hard. We all have days when we feel like staying in bed rather than going to work. We all have days when we don't want to jog down the street, just as we all have days when we would rather be somewhere else than with our significant other. Yet connecting this concept of strength, steadiness, and flexibility to some of life's most difficult decisions makes them easier.

When we are dealing with bringing a relative back into our home when our relationship with him or her is not at its best, it is easier to decide what is the right thing to do and then deal with how to do it. It may be in the best interest of the other person to bring them back and then to decide how they are to take responsibility for their actions and fit into the family's daily routines. Likewise, when dealing with a co-worker who is negligent, it may be easier to decide to keep the person on and then figure out how to help him or her to become responsible.

By the way, I once had a student who started missing class. I could have waited until the end of the semester and flunked him, but instead

I decided to confront him early in the course with a simple state-ment—"In order for me to be able to justify passing you, you have to attend every class from now on." The student said, "Okay" and from then on he came to every class. What he did in class was part of what ultimately determined his grade, but at least he was there.

Please feel free to connect this concept of strength, steadiness, and flexibility to things in your own life. For instance, if you're inter-ested in staying healthy, you know you need to exercise. This is the left hand. The kind of exercise you do is the right hand—it can be swimming, jogging, or a host of other activities. You may also be con-necting this concept to work—such as you have to show up whether it is in person or online. In other words, you can't be absent without permission for any significant amount of time. What you do on the job is flexible—you can have high profile days and you can have days when you're just trying to catch up. Applying this concept to a rela-tionship is similar. You can't ignore it for long periods of time and ex-pect it to be there when you return. How you pay attention to it depends on the relationship—it may be with cuddling, it may be tex-ting, or it may be just hanging out together.

Breaking Tasks Down Into Manageable Steps And Using A Day Planner

I think it was Lee Iacoca, chairman of the Chrysler Corporation be-tween 1979 and 1992, who said, "I can do anything for twenty minutes." This saying has become an inspiration for me because when I break tasks into twenty-minute segments, I can do just about anything.

For instance, cooking a truly outstanding meal for twelve people is not easy, but I can do it when I break it down. My first step is to se-lect a cookbook. True, I have many, but knowing the kind of guests we're expecting, I know the kind of food they will appreciate. For a dinner party just recently, I picked Patrick O'Connel's *The Inn at Little Washington Cookbook.*

The second step I take is to select one recipe for each of the following: appetizer, soup, salad, entree, and desert. I have a piece of paper beside me on the kitchen table on which I jot down the names of the recipes I think might work. I often select recipes I've tried before, especially ones that have worked well. By the way, it helps that when I try a recipe for the first time, I write in the cookbook about how it went so I can remember what to do the next time I make it, especially if I'm making it for guests.

My third step is to make a list of the items I need to buy at the grocery store. My fourth step is to go to the store and buy them. The fifth step is to return home and decide which recipe I need to make first, which second, etc. Yes, it may take me all day, but because I'm doing things step by step, I end up with a great meal that I've really enjoyed making and one that my guests love eating.

By the way, for me it's really important that I separate planning from doing. Both are in and of themselves difficult enough, but together they can be overwhelming.

In addition to breaking large projects down into manageable steps and writing out what I need to do as I mentioned earlier, I also find it helpful to use a day planner. Some items in my planner are obligatory such as "English 309" that I place at 10:30 AM on Tuesday and Thursday each week of the semester I'm teaching. Other items are optional such as "vacuum trunk of car." Putting that off another day or more doesn't matter.

I find it very satisfying to cross off an item once I've finished it. In fact, I do now do what I've seen others do—I add an item to the planner if it has come up unexpectedly and then I cross it off. Recently a student came to my office during office hours and after he left I wrote in my day planner, "Conference with Daniel" and crossed it off. I found that very satisfying.

If, at the end of the day, I haven't had a chance to do something yet want to re-schedule it for the next day, I once again enter it in into my day planner.

If you are the type of person who is by nature organized, right now you're probably thinking—"Duh!" For you, this is what you've done for years and you cannot imagine your life without these things. I've met some people, however, including some students, who struggle with organizing their lives so much so that they have trouble getting things done that are absolutely essential. For them, life is a constant struggle.

So, if you're having trouble organizing your day, try breaking tasks down into 20 minute segments, use a day planner or something in which to list your tasks and cross them off one by one as you do them. Yes, initially this may feel very uncomfortable for you because it's not what you're used to. If so, acknowledge your feeling of discomfort, label it, and let it go—over and over and over. At the end of the day, sit back and review what you've accomplished—just look at it. Breathe in, breathe out.

For now, please take a moment to jot down one of your larger tasks then break it into segments of twenty minutes. Feel free to do this task one segment at a time and later cross off each item as you complete it. In addition, if you don't have a day planner, please consider buying one or creating one of your own. Again, map out your tasks for the upcoming week and cross them off in your day planner as you complete them.

Learning What We're Good At

One thing all good teachers do is to help their students both to identify what they're good at and to then develop these traits even further. Each week my students write one piece, bring it to class to share with members of their response group, and then give it to me. I read them, write specific comments on their drafts and general comments in their folders, and at the beginning of the next class when I return their writings to them I hold a mini-conference with each student. One of the things I make sure I include in both my written and spoken comments is pointing out what I think each student has done well and I say such things as, "This is a great topic—very timely," or "I thought I knew about your topic but I learned so much from this piece." Over time, my students (and I) learn what they're good at and we establish these things as a foundation on which to develop other skills.

My students are in college and because of the outstanding teachers they've had in their K-12 education, some of them already know what they're good at in their writing, but not all of them. One student, for example, had never been told that he wrote really engaging openings and never thought about it himself.

When I was in kindergarten, apparently I told my classmates that I had an elephant in my garage. I remember standing with my teacher and my mom and after my teacher recounted what I had told my classmates, she added, "Donald has a very active imagination." I was five at the time and her comment has stuck with me ever since. My parents had never told me that, although I'm sure they knew and if my teacher had not told me, it might have been a very long time before someone told me or I learned it on my own.

I came across an article a short while ago co-authored by Todd Kashdan, one of my colleagues at George Mason. The title of the article, "A dynamic approach to psychological strength development and intervention," advocates that psychologists go beyond the 'identify and use' approach with their clients to cultivating their clients' strengths even further "through enhanced awareness, accessibility, and effort." One thing I really like about this article is that it supports what I do in my teaching and in my own life. For instance, I encourage my students who already know how to write a good opening to look at the openings of other writers so that they can develop their skills even further. And in the case of my knowing I have an active imagination, I have developed it further by periodically writing short stories.

One of the things that has surprised me when I read Todd's article was what the authors said on page 108. According to another study "…only one-third of people can identify their own strengths (Hill, 2001) and that only 17% of people say they use their strengths 'most of the time' each day (Buckingham, 2007)." However, the more I thought about it, the more it made sense. As I said, if I had not told one of my students that he wrote engaging openings, he may never have known.

Before proceeding further, I want to distinguish between the words strength and strengths. Strength is how strong we are doing one thing or another; strengths are our traits that we're good at. The point I want to make here is that not only is it important that we know what our strengths are, it's also important to know that we can strengthen each one even further.

Now back to the article. Apparently, the mere identification of our strengths brings us increased happiness and decreased depression. This makes sense. Self-knowledge leads to happiness and learning that we are good at something can help us to make wise decisions that further lead to happiness.

Please take a few minutes to jot down the things you're good at. Keep this list within reach for the next few days and add to it if other things come mind.

The Steadiness of Paying Attention

I don't have ADD and I've never had any trouble staying focused, but after I started meditating, my ability to pay attention deepened. At first, it did not occur to me to make the connection (thanks to my habit of compartmentalized thinking), but after a while other people complimented me and only then did it occur to me that there might be a cause/effect relationship. The other change I noticed was a deepening of my ability to listen to people. Not only was it easier, I also enjoyed it more. Sometimes the other person would apologize for rambling on and I would say, "Not at all. I really like listening to you." And I was being honest.

My own experience was backed up a few years ago by a study conducted at the University of Wisconsin in Madison led by Richard Davidson, professor of psychology and psychiatry at that university. As noted by Sandra Blakeslee in her article on Davidson's research, previous studies had shown that meditation increases gray matter, improves the immune system, reduces stress, and promotes a sense of well being. This study was the first, however, to prove that meditation also improves attention. Daniel Levison, one of the staff researchers in the psychology department at the University of Wisconsin who also took part in the study, said, "I'm a much better listener. I don't get lost in my own personal reaction to what people are saying."

My guess is that the practice of paying attention to one's breath and letting go of thoughts not only strengthens attention, it also becomes a habit. When we are listening to someone whose comments are inappropriately negative, meditators pretty much label those comments as such and return their focus to the next thing the other person is saying. For meditators, this is just a habit—nothing special.

We all like sitting down with a good listener and perhaps even more importantly, we love it when we are that good listener listening to ourselves. Over time we come to appreciate the complexity of the situation we are dealing with and when we listen to ourselves with love and compassion, we so appreciate the peace that follows. Knowing we can train ourselves to pay attention to ourselves and others is freeing. We are not bound by our previous levels of attention.

I'm fully aware that for some of us, paying attention is enormously difficult. We're constantly interrupting ourselves and others, we're always comparing and, as the saying goes, "We're all over the place."

Please take a few minutes to describe the way you typically pay attention. If your mind tends to wander, say so. If you tend to stay focused for long periods of time, also say so. Then see if there is anything you can do to let go of distractions in your head in order to increase your ability to pay attention.

Biology Is Stronger Than Psychology

When I was around thirty-five, I began having periods when I felt mildly depressed and I couldn't explain them. My life was no different from the way it had been before. I was healthy and happy overall, I loved my job, family, and friends and I was constantly learning new things, but from time to time I would just feel mentally and emotionally yucky. It was never bad enough to see a doctor, but I did surprise myself when I started to relate to Salinger's Holden Caufield and other depressed characters in the literature I was reading.

Then one day I read an article in *Prevention Magazine* that my late wife had all of a sudden subscribed to. The article talked about how B vitamin deficiencies could lead to feeling stressed, anxious, and depressed. I had no idea if I had a B vitamin deficiency or not, but I thought it was worth a try so I bought a bottle of B-Complex vitamins and began taking them. Within two weeks, the intermittent feelings of depression disappeared. I took B-Complex vitamins every day until a few years ago when I decided to see if they were still the cause of my feeling good about life and sure enough, after two weeks of going off of them, the same downer feelings returned and when I went back on the B-Complex vitamins, those feelings disappeared.

I have to admit that there is a part of me that wants to think that psychology is stronger than biology. I spend almost an hour each day writing in my journal, exercising, and meditating in order to have a healthy and happy life—yet without that little pill each morning, those yucky feelings return.

I first heard the term "biology is stronger than psychology" when my late wife was in the early stages of her brain cancer. She was trying to come up with a reason she had gotten the cancer and even wondered if her bumping her head against a board on her way down into the basement could have caused it. Then one day my son, John, who is a doctor, said that if you have two of one kind of gene, you will not get brain cancer. If you have one of one kind and one of another, you may get it and if you have two of the bad ones, you will get it regardless of how you live your life. It was then that he said, "Biology is stronger than psychology."

The reason I'm including this idea here is that there are times when we need to be aware that we are not always the cause of what we're doing and we're not always responsible for the things that happen to us or how we feel. The important thing is to know when we're responsible and when we're not.

This may sound obvious, but it's important that we have a yearly physical, that we follow up with the proper medications that our doctor may prescribe, and that we become as informed as we can about any conditions that influence our biological health. Medicine is a huge and complex field, one that is constantly changing. Keeping up to date on the areas that affect us directly is part of bringing peace to ourselves and others.

Take a minute to jot down things in your physical life that have an influence on your emotional and spiritual lives. Then list the things in your emotional and spiritual lives that you would like to improve and do your research to see if there is anything you can do in your physical life that might improve things. Obviously, also feel free to speak with your doctor about these things.

158.12 Gal
Gallehr, Donald.
Be gentle : ten ways to bring peac
to yourself and others

3 - 22   6

9 781646 107919